WHEN THE STARS
Towards An Authentic R'

"In the decades since H. P. Lovecraft's untimely death, countless objects, films, novels, stories, and poems have expanded upon The Old Man of Providence's oeuvre and its associated pantheon of alien god-things. Among those secondary creations, alongside such nameless horrors as plush Cthulhus and stranger things, have been numerous false *Necronomicons*, promising arcane wisdom and occult power, but too-often turning out to be a gamut of unpronounceable gobbledygook and a handful of incomprehensible rituals borrowing heavily from Buckland, Crowley, and Spare.

No longer. Canadian author, editor, and poet Scott R. Jones eschews such fannish faux-cult nonsense by approaching Old Grandpa Theobald's life's work and literary legacy as a true spiritual seeker, and, as a result, uncovers real spiritual truths. This is no Simon *Necronomicon*, no coy cash-in; instead, the book you hold in your hands is a sort of Cosmic Horror *How to Win Friends and Influence Cultists*, filled with potentially life-changing wisdom, provocative observation, and beautiful madness. *When the Stars Are Right* is the first real self-help book for the weird fiction crowd."
— Ross E. Lockhart, editor of *The Book of Cthulhu*

"Lovecraft has endured a great deal of violence to his name, his reputation, and his legacy over the years, not all of it undeserved but the particular violence that Mr. Jones has wrought upon him is a thing to behold ... *When the Stars Are Right* is not a book; it's a crime scene. We are invited to watch the crime take place and are made accomplices in the act, following Mr. Jones as he not only carries out this crime but tells how he will accomplish it and then serves us up the cadaver in delicious morsels that we swallow with every turn of the page, knowing we should tell someone, anyone, but not sure if they will even believe us.

For devotees of an atheist, Lovecraft's followers can come across as dogmatic and unyielding as any Barnstomping Baptist and Mr. Jones delights in slitting the throats of every one of their sacred cows all while somehow remaining more true than should be considered a good thing. So read this book, safe in the knowledge that you will enjoy the journey into darkness, just know that it may not be the same you that comes out the other side nor, perhaps, should it be."
— Leeman Kessler, *AskLovecraft.com*

"*When The Stars Are Right* represents a nascent kind of thinking about R'lyehian spirituality ... Jones' work here is, in essence, not to write [a] mysterious, inscrutable *gospel* ... but rather to write a functional *theology*. He has less in common with a St. Peter or a Muhammad (peace be upon them) than he does with, say, Augustine or Jerome or Pope Gregory the Great. His job is not ... to churn out new images from the beyond, but to engage with what has already been given, and to discern from it (as in Pope Gregory's exegesis) what it really means to draw one's spirituality out of somebody else's writing, and how that ought to be done, and what we must understand about it in order to do so. This is serious work; that he has done it at all suggests that we ought to take R'lyehian spirituality a little more seriously. That he has done it well demands it."
— Luke R. J. Maynard

"*When The Stars Are Right* constitutes an important contribution to Weird literature. At points profound, perverse, and personal, Jones provides a reading of the Mythos that reclaims the horror and cosmic strangeness, contradictions and all, framing them as a journey along a dreamer's path, deep among infinitely

inexpressible wonders. This book comes at a critical point in space and time as Lovecraft's literary legacy expands globally. As one might expect, this work frequently dances on the edge of madness and genius. But it boldly contemplates the life-changing notions that chortled and skittered along the edges of Lovecraft's best work. Highly recommended, but don't expect any gates to close easily afterwards"
—Bryan Thao Worra, NEA Fellow in Literature, author of *DEMONSTRA*

"Sly, intelligent, and darkly entertaining, Jones gives Ligotti a run for his money in the Cosmic Horror Philosophy arms race."
—Laird Barron, author of *The Croning* and *The Beautiful Thing That Awaits Us All*

"With this book Scott R. Jones manages to transcend the mire of pseudo-*Necronomicons* and the pop Cthulhu cottage industry. *When the Stars are Right* is a stirring examination of the genuine Darkness that churns not only in the mythos of H.P. Lovecraft but in the universe at large."
—Richard Gavin, author of *At Fear's Altar* and *The Darkly Splendid Realm*

WHEN THE STARS ARE RIGHT:
Towards An Authentic R'lyehian Spirituality

Scott R Jones

Martian Migraine Press
print edition 2014

WHEN THE STARS ARE RIGHT:
Towards An Authentic R'lyehian Spirituality

Cover and interior illustrations © Michael Lee Macdonald
Cover design, interior layout & typesetting © Martian Migraine Press
Author photograph © Derek Ford Photography

National Library of Canada Cataloguing in Publication Data

Jones, Scott R. / 1972 -
When The Stars Are Right: Towards An Authentic
R'lyehian Spirituality / Scott R. Jones

ISBN 978-0-9879928-8-8 (paperback)
ISBN 978-0-9879928-9-5 (electronic book)

martianmigrainepress.com

Printed and bound in Canada

for Meridian

Table of Contents

Foreweird

*Z*um *Raum wird hier die Zeit.* "Time becomes space, here."
  I shall let the above words of Gurnemanz from Wagner's *Parsifal* serve as a warning. I think it only fair. As an additional caution, I should inform you that I am writing this while wearing a tweed jacket, with patches on the elbows and everything. This should explain the German and the Greek, and the Latin, if it comes to it. Very well, then.

In this book, Jones is careful to say *R'lyehian*, rather than *Lovecraftian*, which is to say he inhabits a *topos*, not a *corpus*. This is not Lovecraft's world-view (atheistic, mechanical and absent of meaning), but rather the view of Lovecraft's world (cyclopean, fecund and squamous). To this latter world I bring with me my own biases: those of a Gnostic, a theologian, and a Jungian.

Some 2200 years ago in Alexandria, certain groups of Hellenized (toga-wearing, Greek-speaking) Jews, living in ancient Egypt on the doorstep of the Roman Empire, began producing a kind of cross-cultural cosmogenic fan-fiction; soaring epics of metaphor and argument relating to the nature of humanity, of divinity, of the origin of evil and the monstrous culpability of fate. Because the point of all this authorship was the illumination and examination of *gnosis* - that primal and experiential "knowledge of the heart" (Quispel) – these diverse philosopher-poets have come to be known as the Gnostics. For those familiar with Gnostic literature, there is little doubt that Lovecraft did, however unintentionally, tap into the *urgrund und urbild*

(Tillich) of Gnostic cosmology. Taking "ignorance is bliss" to its inevitable, uncomfortable counterpoint.

For the Gnostics, the *kosmos* ("system") was firmly in the grip of the Archons ("rulers") who were either monstrously sadistic or apathetically incompetent. Fallen angels, grotesque in their ambition and near-limitless in the power over mortals; powers of ignorance, of amnesia, of decay. This is a theme familiar to anyone with a Miskatonic University bumper sticker (Go 'Pods!).

"And the archons created seven powers for themselves, and the powers created for themselves six angels for each one until they became 365 angels. And these are the bodies belonging with the names: the first is Athoth, he has a sheep's face; the second is Eloaiou, he has a donkey's face; the third is Astaphaios, he has a hyena's face; the fourth is Yao, he has a serpent's face with seven heads; the fifth is Sabaoth, he has a dragon's face; the sixth is Adonin, he had a monkey's face; the seventh is Sabbede, he has a shining fire-face… But Yaltabaoth had a multitude of faces, more than all of them." – *Apocryphon of John* (Wisse trans.)

Chaos figures prominently in Gnostic cosmogonies; particularly the dichotomy of "the chaos of nothing" and "the chaos of something". The dynamic tension in Lovecraft's work is the return of somethingness to nothingness, and the insignificance of our ego-identities in this process. There is rarely destruction in Lovecraft, but rather there are undoings. His apocalypse, heralded by Nyarlathotep, is that reality sort of *unhappens*. Lovecraft whimpers, cringes against the dying of the light. While this unmaking is rooted in the realm of horror, its apprehension can also be likened to the beauty of a Tibetan sand mandala – intricate, myriad patterns, made somehow more poignant, more beautiful, because of their temporary nature.

But until that point of unmaking, we deal with Chaos: The present determining the future, although the approximate present failing to approximately determine the future. Things tend toward the weird. Dynamic systems such as the Archonic kosmos are sensitive to initial conditions, and the Great Old Ones in this context are archetypal initial conditions. Our ideas – all these clean Platonic vertices and tidy Euclidean planes – originate from squelching glands, tendrils of synapse, all using inelegant, asymmetrical squirming proteins as a medium of communication for what is ultimately energy. Chaos talking to itself, emerging through us, although through an aspect of us we rarely recognize and quite advisingly refute.

*Not for a moment dare we succumb
to the illusion that an archetype can
be finally explained and disposed of.*

— CG Jung, *The Psychology of the Child Archetype
[Das göttliche Kind]* (1941)

So here is an attempt at a coherent theology – perhaps more properly a cryptarchaeoxenotheology (the study of hidden, ancient, and alien gods) – of Lovecraft's mythos, knowing full well that a rational exploration of the archetypal is, at best, a temporary and disposable scaffolding while we construct something more valuable from experience and not criticism. This is true of the serious consideration of any body of literature – insights of equal value (albeit different flavours) can be arrived at via Shakespeare, or Tolkien, or Lessing, or Dr. Seuss, all roads leading to Rome, as it were. One can accept this process as a thought experiment, a writing prompt, or something with which one can ultimately identify. As you like.

Theologically, the only omission here seems to be Azathoth, which is the teleological *raison d'être* of the whole affair. Ontogeny recapitulates phylogeny and all that; and from this mad, blind nothingness comes all the mad, blind nothingnesses of the R'lyehian undertaking – qlipothic kin to the *mushin no shin*, mind-of-no-mind, of Zen Buddhism.

*...outside the ordered universe that amorphous
blight of nethermost confusion which blasphemes
and bubbles at the center of all infinity — the
boundless daemon sultan Azathoth, whose
name no lips dare speak aloud, and who
gnaws hungrily in inconceivable, unlighted
chambers beyond time and space amidst the
muffled, maddening beating of vile drums and
the thin monotonous whine of accursed flutes.*

— H. P. Lovecraft, *The Dream Quest of
Unknown Kadath*

*... the monstrous nuclear chaos beyond angled
space which the Necronomicon had mercifully
cloaked under the name of Azathoth.*

— H. P. Lovecraft, *The Whisperer in Darkness*

In its place Jones posits Yog Sothoth; though it would seem this archetype is more of an *experiential* aspect of Azathoth, a compression of chaos,
an event-horizon of Azathoth. If Yog Sothoth is Wheeler's quantum foam,
or even a ghastly santorum froth of excrement and blood, of semen and pet-
rochemicals, it is still only a nothing defined by a something; with Azathoth
as the *potential* for the foam, the *logos* of it. Yog Sothoth would seem to be
the demiurge which assembles the experiential, material universe, and yet
is forever separated from its ideal, its blueprint, however incomprehensible.
The workman trudges on, while the architect is notably absent, ignorant,
and insane.

In the black-earth / red-earth binary of early Egyptian theology, it may
be surprising to realize that the ancient Egyptians did not worship gods *per
se*. They instead spoke of *names*, the *netjeru*, the word being depicted by an
upright axe. Osiris, Isis, Horus (as the Greeks called them millennia later)
were names of something, the *same* something, and not necessarily things
unto themselves. Likewise does Lovecraft give us the Great Old Ones: not
tentacled kaiju from the depths of a physical sea, but narrative-arc-deviating
singularities or ill-behaved compressions of ideal form; thusly;

> Singularities
> of being: Yog Sothoth
> of meaning: Nyarlathotep
> of manifestation: Shub-Niggurath
> of identity: Dagon; the amphibious traveler
> between conscious and subconscious realms.

Thus the quantum world, the semiotic world, the genetic world, and the
individual world.

All of this is at first rather inaccessible – hence Lovecraft's famously
vague, unnamable, indecipherable, indescribable, incomprehensible adjec-
tives. Jones notes that the only anthropomorphic entity in HPL's work is its
most iconic:

Cthulhu.

Cthulhu in his pop-culture *kaiju* form is merely Gabriel's trumpet, the
cock-crow of dawn. As with most apocalypse fantasies, it is the province of
the adolescent. There will be an upheaval of the old order, and the new order

shall have carte blanche on which to impose itself – every teenager wishing fervently her parents would go away for the weekend. This is in no way a condemnation: each phase in psychological and spiritual evolution is necessary and cannot be skipped over. But this brings us only to the human, and not to the R'lyehian. Ultimately, this entirely comprehensible chibi-thulhu is a kind of whistling past the graveyard.

No, the Cthulhu of interest here is in his role of Morpheus, the Dreamer. It's this navigator of the great currents of nocturnal experience and license that appeals and transforms. In other words, big rubbery dragon-winged Cthulhu fixed in space and time, can devour only a finite number of cultists in a single sitting ("Yum Yum!"). However, to the R'lyehian, the vastly unquantifiable and archetypal Dream-Cthulhu is in every human (and non-human) imagination. Waiting. Always. Everywhere.

> *The dream is the small hidden door in the deepest and most intimate sanctum of the soul, which opens to that primeval cosmic night that was soul long before there was conscious ego and will be soul far beyond what a conscious ego could ever reach.*
>
> — CG Jung, *The Meaning of Psychology for Modern Man (1934)*

So the Madness of Cthulhu is not clinical dysfunction or psychosis, but a hermeneutic suspension of the pedestrian, rational mind that is required to successfully navigate the waking world. In its place is the supra-rational, the information that comes without the need for communication, egoic disassociation, the disintermediated experience of experience. What Jones refers to here as the Black Gnosis.

If I were to tell you I actually saw a beautifully strange city emerge from the sea, and in its seeing that I gained deep insight into my own psyche, you would have reasonable grounds to demand physical evidence or else have me institutionalized. Yet if I told you I dreamt this, and because of this dream I gained these same insights, you would no doubt nod and take another sip of your coffee. In our Nietzschean age of mechanistic meaninglessness, flensed horses and droning Dawkinistas, where the machine has been scrubbed clean of any ghosts; dreams, apparently, are granted a certain pass.

You can take your head apart with this book if you like, but you will never get it back together again. Unlike the sophomoric tattoo-parlour-flash of Carroll, the lunatic-trickster Bertiaux, or the almost-brilliant Grant – not to mention the gap-toothed carny antics of LaVey, whose Aynrandian quotes are eagerly nodded along-to by Creationist tea-partiers – Jones is not so easy to dismiss.

You have already passed a gate, by possessing this book and by reading thus far in its introduction. There's a specific resonance or remnant of reminiscence that's curiously cavorting about your cortex, the drumming of dreams in the distant dark. Give in. As Thompson said, when the going gets weird, the weird turn pro. Time to correlate your contents and get your HR Geiger counter ticking. But remember,

time becomes space here.

Jordan Stratford
October 2013

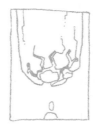

Sunken Bells in the Deep:
An Introduction

Why write a book on R'lyehian spirituality?

When I first began talking about *When The Stars Are Right*, the question I would encounter the most, at least in certain circles, was not *what is R'lyehian spirituality?* but *why would you feel the need to write such a thing?* Among members of a growing geek culture, the crazed cults, madness-inducing magical tomes, and hideous alien monster-gods of Howard Phillips Lovecraft's fictional world (commonly referred to as the *Cthulhu Mythos*) have achieved a kind of pop-cultural apotheosis: the image of the Oozing Tentacle is now, in the second decade of the 21st Century, the visual cipher for creeping, malevolent evil, replacing the Dripping Claw/Teeth or the Red Horn.

This is in no small part due to the massive amount of entertainment products spawned from the febrile depths of the Cthulhu Mythos: to the reams of literary and not-so-literary material still generated each year, we must add role-playing games, comic books, radio dramas, podcasts, clothing, studio-grade as well as independent films and animations, and of course, plush dolls[1]. For my peers and associates, as embedded in Lovecraft's culture

---

1   Touching on this same point in his essay "Cthulhu's Polymorphous Perversity" (*Cthulhurotica*, 2010, Dagan Books), author and Lovecraftian scholar Kenneth Hite comments on the *Buddy 'Thulhu* action figure: "a parody of director Kevin Smith's

as I, the question *what is R'lyehian spirituality?* is the less important one, as constant exposure to the tropes, memes and themes of the Mythos have given us, if not a specific answer, at least an admittedly nebulous idea of what such a spiritual practice might look like.

But then, it's the ubiquity of these very ideas, vague and multiform as they are, that creates the question I was asked most: *why write such a thing?* I'll be the first to admit that no one needs another fake Necronomicon, another Lovecraftian bestiary, another working (or not-working, as the case may be) spell book of cobbled-together Sumerian magic and breathless kabbalistic calisthenics. Legitimate magicians working in the hoary old Thelemic and modern Chaos and Vodoun traditions[1] alike, and pseudo-Satanic American charlatans[2] have thoroughly mined that vein, and, in the case of the latter, done so almost beyond the point of useful parody.

Why write a book on R'lyehian spirituality? The answer, for me, is simple.

Because it has not yet been written.

What you are holding in your hands is not a grimoire, a Simonomicon, a smirking call to tongue-in-cheek culthood, a post-modern hoax text, a

---

satire of the modern Church's *Buddy Christ* travesty of Jesus" (in the film *Dogma*) which is "so semiotically weightless that it actually floats away of its own accord."

1   Phil Hine's *The Pseudonomicon*, Kenneth Grant's Typhonian books, Peter Carrol's *Liber Null* and *Psychonaut*, and Michael Bertiaux's *The Voduon Gnostic Workbook* are all excellent volumes for the practicing R'lyehian interested in the serious magical expression of a Lovecraftian worldview.

2   Derrick Dishaw, a strange and awful little man from Wisconsin who calls himself by the name "Venger Satanis" is the high priest, Ipssisimus and leader of his own self-styled 'Cult of Cthulhu': a marginally Satanic organization (liberally and literally doused in cut-rate Eldritch Ichor) which is not in actuality affiliated in any way with the real Church of Satan. (I'm given to understand that the august association wants nothing to do with him.) I was made aware of Dishaw's Lovecraftian "bibles" about three-quarters of the way through the penning of this work, and it would be more than fair to state that I was thoroughly appalled. The books are a delusional farrago of plagiarized Wikipedia entries, adolescent Nietzschean rantings, misogynistic tirades and disturbingly serious endorsements of "ritual murder". It is not even clear whether or not the 'Cult of Cthulhu' should be considered a parody, so muddled is the message. I hesitate to direct anyone to Mr Dishaw's particularly lurid corner of the Internet (and this for the offense it can do to the eyeballs alone) but for those with the stomach for bad design and worse thinking, www.cultofcthulhu.net reads as a primer for how not to practice as a R'lyehian. Not recommended, but perhaps educational after all: there but for the grace of Dagon go we all.

scholarly study of Lovecraft and his philosophy, or even a critique of his literary output.

When The Stars Are Right is a collection of essays and meditations that point towards an authentic R'lyehian spirituality: what it looks like, how it feels, how it is perceived from within and from without the experience. It is an attempted mapping of a genuine (and genuinely understood) Lovecraftian belief system *sans* Lovecraft and the worst excesses of his one-note followers. It is a stripping of the pop-cultural trappings from the glowing naked form of the Mythos. It is Cthulhu without the glib tentacle-jab to the ribs. It is the Three-Lobed Burning Eye locking onto your own, steady, unwavering, never delivering the absolution of a knowing wink.

Some of the following essays are purely speculative, others auto-biographical and philosophical. There are examinations of the Great Old Ones as emergent properties of certain types of consciousness; meditations on shifting conceptual city-scapes and the beneficial aspects of multiple personality disorder; notes on pan and omni-sexuality, a brief discussion of anti-natalism, and finally, ruminations on the nature of death, time, and becoming. *When The Stars Are Right* is, essentially, an auto-ethnographical text: not a manual of practice, a defense of the beliefs herein, or an attempt at apologetics. It is a report from the crinkly fractal front lines of conscious-ness. A dispatch from the edge of That Which Is.

Of course, the question of *why write such a thing?* leads naturally to another: *why do I feel qualified to write it?* What makes *Scott R Jones* the par-ticular intersection of mind and matter, flesh and feeling, personality and perspective, to build such a textual artifact? The answer, again, is simple.

I have felt the Call.

Yes, *that* one.

I first felt it a full six years before ever encountering the fiction of Howard Phillips Lovecraft. And, appropriately enough, I felt it in my dreams.

I was fourteen, maybe fifteen years old. I've always been a great, vivid, Technicolor dreamer, the sort that wakes up of a morning exhausted by a night's worth of excessive oneiric activity. My dreams never repeated though, at least, not until that first night.

I awoke into the dream swiftly, without preamble, without surreal narra-tive introduction. I awakened into the dream and found myself standing at the edge of a barren cliff. A glance behind revealed a hammered sheet of sand and bare, dusty stone that stretched to the limit of my sight. The view ahead was similarly flat and massive: the sea, the western sea (for somehow I knew I faced that direction), insistently wore away at the base of the cliff. This was a place of boundaries, of drawn, stepped horizons: the lifeless land of sand

and stone, the cliff edge where I stood; below, the cliff base, the shoreline, and below that, further along the curve of the earth, the edge where sea met sky, leagues away. I breathed deeply, tested the air with my tongue. Salt and ancient decay; strange fragrance as of scorched metal resting on stiff shelves of breeze. Each line, I felt, each boundary was straining to break with the force that moved along its edge, seeking weakness. I stood still upon the cliff as small eternities accumulated around me like nautaloid fossils.

Then, on the western horizon before me, a cataclysm. I cannot see it clearly, the distance is too great, but at the crack between the worlds of water and air, some titanic event occurs. A small moon, dejected and suicidal, launched from its cold velvet perch and fell. A long-sunken continent heaved itself up from the ocean floor, weed-choked and triumphant, shaking off the corpses of whales and the slime of millennia. A great sundering thing, an oneiric bomb, separating dream-elements one from the other. An irredeemable shattering. I am terrified, fascinated, deathly ill, in love.

From this point on the horizon, from out of the tumult and froth, there is now a rushing. A force, an energetic fusion as of gravity and cold glee, speeds eastward, towards the shore, the cliff. Towards me. I can feel its rushing; I answer its eagerness with my own. My nerves sing and my eyeballs dance in their sockets, my hands reach out, the knuckles cracking and multiplying, my fingers lengthening impossibly in their anguish to touch.

The cataclysm is so far off, beyond sight, yet the speed of the rushing thing that was birthed there is so great that I know, I *know*, that to see it finally appear like a diamond point on the line of the horizon is to have it upon me in the next instant.

And for six nights in a row, I awoke before that instant. A true awakening as well, as abrupt a change of state, of consciousness, as I have ever experienced. The feeling of ecstatic access, of breaking through into something beyond the standard dream source material, was overwhelming. The first night was amazing, the second troubling. By the time I awoke from the dream on the third night, I was thoroughly disturbed. Nights Four through Six I spent in a near fever of post-dream sleeplessness, flavoured with a potent mix of dread and what I can only describe as a kind of dark joy, a negative exaltation.

It was on the sixth night that I decided to write the dream down.

Now, on the surface, this would seem a reasonable course of action. Many people keep a dream journal. Upon closer examination though, the motivation to record the contents of the dream falls apart. This decision is, for me, the penultimate weirdness of the experience. Here was a dream that, from its first appearance, had gouged itself into my memory, and subsequent replays had only deepened the groove. This was not something I would *ever* forget. Even today (in my fortieth year) I can recall it with migraine clarity: the feel of stone beneath my feet, the smell of the air. I did not *need* to write it down.

Nevertheless, before sleep on the seventh night, I set aside a notebook on the nightstand. A pen. Another pen, in case the first ran out of ink. A pencil, in case *both* pens ceased to function. The absurdity of this activity was lost on me at the time. Clearly, there were forces at work. This is a foundation lesson of R'lyehian spirituality: there are always forces at work.

Again, I did not need to write the dream down. And the first pen worked just fine.

The dream progressed as before. The instant arrived, the moment when my dream self would perceive the rushing thing as it cleared the line of the western horizon, appearing as a glittering spear-point targeted for the space between my eyes. The force filled my awareness; it was *upon me* in every sense of the term. In many ways, it still is...

I awoke, or dreamed that I did, and reached for the paper and pen in the dark. At high speed, I filled a half-dozen pages with scrawl, with what I thought (in my barely conscious, threshold state) were the contents of the dream. Which, in retrospect, may have been. Exhausted, finally, the pen dropped from my hand and I fell away into dreamless black.

In the morning... ah, but in the morning! In the morning, madness and the hasty burning of those pages. In the morning, fervent prayers to the god of my father's (a standard Old Testament demiurge type passed through a proto-Baptist filter), sick twistings of anxiety and fear in the pit of my stomach, for in the morning?

In the morning my eyes fell on those half-dozen pages and saw not a record of the dream, in English, written in my own hand, but a mass of closely packed, incomprehensible symbols and scratchings that nevertheless showed evidence of structure, distinct letter-forms, actual syntax. In my own hand. On that morning, everything changed.

The years since then have seen the symbiotic relationship with the Other (possession? autonomous ego splinter?) I encountered that night grow, deepen and become much more complex. The script has been analyzed nearly to death, subjected to code breaking techniques and cipher manipulations, all to no avail: whatever it may or may not be (sacred text or laundry list), whatever it has to tell, whatever "truths" it may contain, it has proven to be one thing, certainly and above all else, and that is *resistant*. Fifteen years, one marriage, one divorce, one conversion experience and several spiritual upheavals later, the channeled writing gave way to glossolaliac trances, along with the transmission of bizarre *katas* and torturously fluid *mudras* rapidly executed in the air around me by my own alien-to-me hands. Because of it, this symbiosis, I have been variously the special project and sometime target of occult groups and random so-called magicians of varying levels of professionalism.

On that morning, though, I knew nothing of what was to come. I only knew that something awful had happened to me. Awful in the original sense. For, behind the pre-programmed fundamentalist Christian anxiety I felt, behind the prescribed guilt that was only there because I felt I *should* be feeling it, pulsed a great awe. A terrible, awful knowledge that was not knowledge *per se*, but Knowing: pure and uncontaminated by rationality, by intellectual scaffolding, by my own humanness. It was there, this gnosis, in seed form, and it would take many years of trial and suffering and unalloyed weirdness to bring it to consciousness.

Six years after that morning, I read Howard Phillips Lovecraft for the first time, in the Arkham House collection *Tales of the Cthulhu Mythos* (the 1990 revised edition). As far as I'm able to tell, nothing guided me to that book in the library. It's quite possible that I was merely attracted to the green of the cover, or found the Jeffrey K Potter photo montages illustrating the pages within intriguing. I recall wondering, in my 20 year old naïveté, what the *Divers Hands* in the byline of "H. P. Lovecraft and Divers Hands" meant. Whatever the reason, I withdrew the book from the library, and took it home, and began to read.

I read of books transcribed by desert-addled madmen from the howlings of demons. I read of cults that sought to bring that which dwells Outside *in*. I read of sane people, scholars and rationalists to a man, reduced to gibbering wrecks by revealed truths. I read of indescribably ancient beings, the inhabitants of equally ancient alien cities, transmitting their will and desires through dream and trances. I read of the Call of Cthulhu...

Something stirred within me. In some deep and authentic place inside, a place from which a repeating dream had hammered its way into the waking world, a place where I became not-I, an Eye slid open and did not close again. And a seed once planted began to grow.

I'm qualified to write a book on R'lyehian spirituality because I have been living it, day to day, and through long nights of ecstasy and madness, for twenty-five years. I have no degrees. I am a member of no special order or group or cabal. There is no one above or below me in some ridiculous hierarchy of meaningless rituals and forms-to-be-obeyed.

There is only the Call. Sunken bells tolling in the deep...

Answer them with me.

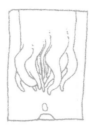

H. P. Lovecraft:
An Acknowledgement,
A Dismissal

If you're reading this book, then it's likely you have the basic biographical background on Howard Phillips Lovecraft, his life and his work. You've read his stories, at the very least, and perhaps even understand his philosophy. Maybe you can rattle off the denizens of the Mythos pantheon and have probably (and literally) bought the t-shirt.

Fritz Lieber famously referred to Lovecraft as "the Copernicus of modern horror"; a man who, tired of the anthrocentric world view of the traditional weird tale (with its narrow focus on vampires, were-beasts, ghosts and other spirits influencing the human sphere), cast his conceptual nets wide into the outer depths of space and time, pulling back from the dark gulfs between the stars horrors difficult to parse, monstrous in their utter alienness, in their exteriority to all things human.

In many ways, his fledgling Mythos and the denizens within was a conceptual and artistic revolution: one of the earliest open-source "sandbox" fictional worlds, Lovecraft laid open his creation to his fellow writers, to dabble with and alter as they pleased, giving rise to a curiously organic structure that has allowed his creations (Arkham, Innsmouth, dark Yuggoth on the Rim) to far outlive the man himself.

It is not my purpose here to repeat Lovecraft's personal history: his mentally-ill parents and unusual childhood, the peculiarities of his education, his nervous disposition, his unfortunate and generally lacklustre love life and sexual relationships, his quirky-by-any-standards Anglophilia, his wildly absurd and quite frankly repugnant (even for its time) racism, his penchant for epistolary communications, or even his writing habits. These areas of Lovecraft's life have already been covered, extensively and with much deep scholarship, by any number of excellent biographers[1].

Nor is it my intention to claim that Lovecraft was in some way a prophet or seer, who in his fiction somehow intuited the existence of the Great Old Ones, acting as an unconscious or semi-conscious priest. It may seem contradictory to state, but Howard Phillips Lovecraft, the man who placed R'lyeh on the map in a very precise sense, was *not*, in fact, R'lyehian. A staunch materialist and avowed nihilist, Lovecraft was as tongue-in-cheek an atheist as any of his latter-day followers. One can easily find, circulating in certain occult circles, the theory or notion that Lovecraft was "right all along" about the Great Old Ones: their characteristics and personalities, their objective existence. This is a tired old chestnut and one I don't wish to parrot here.

I will, however, paraphrase Wittgenstein, and say that Lovecraft was *right enough* on these matters. I leave the details of his Cthulhu Mythos to be hashed out and argued over by those whose only concern *vis a vis* the Great Old Ones is how many sanity points a person would lose if, say, they were to stumble upon a Dark Young of Shub-Niggurath in some sacred woodland, or (in the case of card-carrying occultists) whether Daoloth is best summoned with Sumerian or Akkadian incantations. To obsess in such a way is to miss the point of the Mythos altogether: there *is* a truth that lies behind it, there is real information trapped in the webbing that spans the adjective-scaffolding of Lovecraft's fiction, and between the lines of *The Call of Cthulhu* and *The Silver Key*, phantom realities pulse and writhe, waiting to be actuated by the discerning reader.

No, for our purposes in building an authentic R'lyehian spirituality, we must acknowledge Lovecraft's creative access to deeper truths while at the same time not becoming tied down by his (and others) assuredly limited interpretations of those same truths. We find ourselves in the classic position *vis a vis* creators and their creation: having to separate the man from

---

1 For more biographical information on Lovecraft the man, the excellent (and sometimes contradictory) volumes by L. Sprague deCamp (*Lovecraft: A Biography*, multiple printings by multiple publishers since 1976) and S. T. Joshi (*I Am Providence: The Life and Times of H. P. Lovecraft*, Hippocampus Press, 2010) are essential reading.

the mythos, the sad falseness of a life lived poorly from the enriching truth condensed from that living.

Lovecraft's line of approach to the things he conceived of (things not original to him, surely) was mainly one of attack, seclusion, paranoia and repression. He imagined himself a refined, intelligent man who celebrated a personal aesthetic of racial and intellectual purity, so of course he would dress the radically Outside elements of his fiction in the shifting, amorphous flesh of monsters. All that was squamous, soft, and unnamable: these, for Lovecraft, were the epitome of foulness and evil, though even he took pains to remind his readers of their essential nature as things that were beyond such dualistic terms.

So, though I necessarily borrow from Lovecraft a framework for entering and appreciating the nuances of R'lyehian spirituality, I choose to use it in a manner that is necessarily loose, one that may not jibe with the preconceptions and fixed ideas of some of Lovecraft's more hidebound followers, while at the same time allowing for an appreciation and a certain level of understanding for those who are perhaps not overly familiar with the Mythos. It may actually be beneficial for the reader of this book to have had a limited exposure to Lovecraft's work and its later additions, or even none at all.

A case in point: in a later chapter on Cthulhu, I go beyond the traditional (and woefully popular) "kai-ju terror" interpretation of the Lord of Dreams that Lovecraft himself insisted upon in his eponymous tale, into an appreciation of Cthulhu as a sort of reversed-Platonic ideal of Madness itself. Too often is Cthulhu perceived only in its monstrous aspect, and this view says more about the perceiver than anything else; I venture beyond the unregenerate view, to a place where dark becomes light, and the feeble sanity that defines the world as this-and-so in its quest for order is seen for the illusion it is. Essentially, one wonders whether Lovecraft did not protest too much regarding his gods and beasties, that in fact his deepest (and probably shameful to his effete New England soul) wish was to be torn open, gutted and reshaped by the revelations he so fearfully imagined and put to paper in the night.

Clearly, Lovecraft was a conflicted man, a creator at war with his creation, and his self. It is perhaps this inner conflict, as much as his paranoia and cosmic nihilism, which makes his work resonate today. Lovecraft suffered for his art, true, but mostly he just suffered. He died, penniless and alone, from a combination of cancer of the small intestine and malnourishment. He is buried in Swan Point Cemetery, Providence, Rhode Island.

We thank him for his art, then, and acknowledge the suffering that produced it, even as we leave the man (a random confluence of flesh and foibles, if ever there was one) in the ground.

Or, if we are to be generous (and in a Universe devoid of meaning, why *not* be such?), let us leave Howard Phillips Lovecraft to the Dreamlands he loved so much.

The Deadly Light:
Examining the Great Old Ones

What do we know ... of the world and the universe about us? Our means of receiving impressions are absurdly few, and our notions of surrounding objects infinitely narrow. We see things only as we are constructed to see them, and can gain no idea of their absolute nature. With five feeble senses we pretend to comprehend the boundlessly complex cosmos, yet other beings with a wider, stronger, or different range of senses might not only see very differently the things we see, but might see and study whole worlds of matter, energy, and life which lie close at hand yet can never be detected with the senses we have.

— H. P. Lovecraft, *From Beyond*

To enter into an examination of the Great Old Ones burdened with the all-too-human assumption that they are merely fictional creations of a single human mind is as faulty and blinkered as assuming that they are actual deities. While not denying that, in an infinite universe, the latter is always a possibility, we must acknowledge that, for our purposes and due to our limited powers of observation as human beings with human senses and human minds, there is no way for us to truly apprehend the Great Old Ones as distinct entities, at least, not until that moment when the stars are right and they rise, finally, freed from their conceptual prisons. Prisons which we ourselves, if we are faithful to R'lyehian principles, will be free of as well.

Until that moment, we must content ourselves with an appreciation of the Great Old Ones as emergent properties of R'lyehian consciousness; an ever-increasing density of the fractal connectedness of awareness that is the hallmark of a sorcerous mentality; end-states of the Black Gnosis.

Approaching the Great Old Ones correctly is almost always a problem of scale, and, to a lesser extent, perspective. To Lovecraft, and to the protagonists he modeled after himself, the Great Old Ones were monsters first, aliens second, and only gods insofar as their longevity, indestructibility, technologies, and mastery of sorceries allowed them to be. To Lovecraft, they were the blind, unknowable forces of chaos that shape the universe made otherworldly flesh, composed of matters and energies forever incomprehensible. They were cold, abyssal horror incarnate, and should they be even dimly glimpsed, the results of such a revelation are ever the same...

> *... some day the piecing together of dissociated knowledge will open up such terrifying vistas of reality, and of our frightful position therein, that we shall either go mad from the revelation or flee from the deadly light into the peace and safety of a new dark age.*[1]

Yes, for Lovecraft and his fictional doppelgangers, the Great Old Ones were the original, primal fount of madness: a madness that deranged, a too-bright truth that burned. For humankind, knowledge of the Old Ones and what they represented brought only insanity and death. It should be noted, however, that though presented in the fictions as monsters, the Old Ones were not conceived of as evil in and of themselves. There is little doubt that Lovecraft's peculiar brand of cosmicism was influenced by Nietzsche: his abhorrent beasties were beyond dualistic constructions of Good and Evil.

---

1   *The Call of Cthulhu*, H. P. Lovecraft

Of course contact with the deities of the Mythos results in madness, but only the ignorant look upon the vista that is revealed and pronounce it terrifying. Only the unregenerate would claim that the position of mankind within the grand cosmic schema is frightening, before fleeing back into the dark. So, a revealed truth destroys a previously passionately held falsehood, smashing at the foundations of the all-too-human ego, an ego that coddled itself with cozy monkey certainties? Fine. Revelation drives one mad, but it is revelation still! The light is deadly, but light it remains. In the drive towards truth, who would not endure long cycles of ever-brightening apocalypse? Only the foolish, those who would cling to their own ignorance.

The R'lyehian knows this, and holds it (lightly, lightly, as one would cradle a precious gem or an alien spore) as a prime tenet of his faith. Not for him the peace of ignorance, the safety of small sentience. Though he agrees that the Great Old Ones are monsters, he understands the term in its original Latin sense of *monstrare*, from which we derive the word *demonstrate*, "to show": to know the Old Ones is to have the truth of our existence demonstrated constantly. An interesting comparison here would be with the so-called "wrathful Buddhas" of Tibetan *bon-po* shamanism: aspects of universal constants that necessarily tear the supplicant, body and soul, from his own delusions. The gods of the R'lyehian put him in his place, that frightful, maddening, *true* place, on a daily basis.

So, in examining the nature and essence of the Great Old Ones herein, we will naturally do so from the R'lyehian viewpoint, which has little to do with the perspective of Lovecraft-the-man and perhaps even less with the views of his followers and assorted aficionados of his fiction. Though I will occasionally reference some small paragraph of Lovecraft's writings, I will use them as jumping-off points into R'lyehian thinking, not as gospel.[1]

We will make no distinctions in the following pages between the Great Old Ones and the Outer Gods[2], or which deity is allied with which other deity or cult or servitor race, and we care not a jot for, say, the hit points of a Dark Young of Shub-Niggurath or what sort of sanity loss can be

---

1 A notion Lovecraft himself would have had some trouble with.

2 I've chosen to skip over such deities of the Mythos that serve no function beyond representing some basic principle or event (ie. Azathoth, a deified portrayal of the Big Bang); or, say, Nodens, he of the ridiculously baroque chariot, trident, and vague placement in the pantheon; or any of the multitude of cobbled-together abominations added on in later years by other writers (though I do admit to a fondness for the foul iterations gifted to us by Ramsey Campbell). For our purposes here, I've focused on the conceptual-trinity of Yog-Sothoth/Shub-Niggurath/Nyarlathotep; Cthulhu as a locus for the Black Gnosis and sorcerous consciousness; and Dagon as exemplar of the "maker" aesthetic that is so vital to a R'lyehian lifestyle.

expected during an encounter with a byakhee. These concerns are not the concerns of the R'lyehian; they belong to the dabblers, the faux-cultists and smug atheists (often one and the same creature) who throw up a perimeter wall of words around the placid island of ignorance we all share and then pay tittering, tongue-in-cheek lip-service to *the horrors, the horrors* that lie beyond. They say they enjoy "a good scare", these dilettantes of the dark spaces between the stars. They claim themselves as "searchers after horror", but then allow their search to end at the local used book store, gaming shop, or pagan coffee clatch.

The R'lyehian breaks down that pathetic wall (because, like all walls, it *demands* to be broken down) and launches herself upon those black seas, to sail or swim or sink as the tides decide, for the Great Old Ones are to be *experienced*, felt as living realities, embraced, merged with. We cannot know them as they know themselves, but we must try nevertheless.

The R'lyehian must risk that deadly light, for in its rays she becomes, like the Great Old Ones, serene and primal, undimensioned and unseen.

The Prolonged of Life:
Meditations on Yog-Sothoth

*The Old Ones were, the Old Ones are, and
the Old Ones shall be. Not in the spaces we
know, but between them, they walk serene
and primal, undimensioned and to us unseen.
Yog-Sothoth knows the gate. Yog-Sothoth is
the gate. Yog-Sothoth is the key and guardian
of the gate. Past, present, future, all are one
in Yog-Sothoth. He knows where the Old Ones
broke through of old, and where They shall
break through again ... Yog-Sothoth is the key
to the gate, whereby the spheres meet.*

With this passage from the Necronomicon (quoted in *The Dunwich Horror*), we are introduced to the deity that took the prime position in Lovecraft's pantheon, at least as far as Lovecraft himself was concerned. It was only later compilers and commentators on Lovecraft's *oevré* that assigned Cthulhu's name to the Mythos. In letters written to members of his epistolary circle, Lovecraft continually referenced his work and the growing shared mythic cycle it was spawning as "Yog-Sothothery".

And yet the figure of Yog-Sothoth, like its paramour Shub-Niggurath, makes no real appearance in Lovecraft's fiction. It is merely referenced in *The Dunwich Horror*, as the ultraterrestrial sire of Lavinia Whateley's awful hybrid twins. We never actually meet the father, though, and are instead treated to descriptions of his offspring. In the tale *The Horror in the Museum* (ghost-written by Lovecraft for Hazel Heald), Yog-Sothoth is described as "*only* a congeries of iridescent globes, yet stupendous in its malign suggestiveness"[1]: yet another example of Lovecraft's predilection for the vague descriptor.

Yog-Sothoth's prison (if something of its power and stature could be considered to be prisoned at all) is a sort of dimensional un-zone, outside of the curvature of space-time. It is described as being "coterminous[2] with all Time and Space" and as "the Lurker at the Threshold". Indeed, it could be argued that Yog-Sothoth is "the threshold" itself, the key and guardian of the gate, and the gate: a liminal state-of-being, a limitless boundary. What is a door, a gate? A tool of transitioning, from one space to another, from Inside to Outside; a piece of architecture that makes solid a line drawn in the sand; a something that defines a nothing but which is, in and of itself, nothing *without* that Nothing it defines.

Why is the image of a solitary door standing in the middle of a desert so compelling? For the same reason that Yog-Sothoth, the All-in-One and One-in-All, resonated so deeply with Lovecraft, and continues to resonate with R'lyehian spirituality. It hints at the truth of doors, of gates, and of that which lies beyond them: *everything is permeable.* This is one of the lessons of Yog-Sothoth.

Hollowness and void. Existence is a thing to be entered into, thresholds are there to be crossed, and there are gates everywhere. *Knock and it shall be opened to you,* goes the biblical admonition. The R'lyehian is rarely so polite as to wait for an invitation, though, and actively seeks out keys. But what vistas yawn wide once that door is opened? An examination of Yog-Sothoth's esoteric qualities provides some answer.

And, stripped of the monstrous qualities Lovecraft was fond of dressing his deities in, Yog-Sothoth is very much an esoteric beast.

What are we to make of the "malign suggestiveness" of a collection of "iridescent globes" in the first place? Yog-Sothoth is a very practical nightmare for artists to depict: how does one render a froth of bubbles frightening, or even merely grotesque? Clearly there is something else at work here. What does Yog-Sothoth represent? Its bubbly form recalls the "quantum foam" of the new physics, a sort of frothing zone of pure potential in which all things are embedded; its prison the contortional complexities of 11-dimensional membrane theory. Yog-Sothoth tests the boundaries of all Time and Space; Yog-Sothoth is bounded by all Time and Space; Yog-Sothoth is the boundary itself! A marvelous confusion of manifestation!

---

1 Italics mine

2 Coterminous: (of regions or properties) having matching boundaries; or, adjoining and sharing a boundary.

Yet we'd be remiss to assume that the god is merely an abstract formula or personification of a principle of obscure physics. For there is *life* there: Yog-Sothoth lives and seethes, bleeds across its own demarcation lines and breeds with what it finds on the other sides. It is many-sided, of that we have no doubt. Lovecraft and his co-writer E. Hoffman Price give us a clue in their story *Through the Gates of the Silver Key*.

In that tale, the figure of Randolph Carter (a para-fictional doppelganger for Lovecraft himself) presses beyond our world and into ultra-telluric dimensions (with the aid of the titular Silver Key) in search of Ultimate Truth[1], thus ensuring his eventual contact with the penultimate avatar of Yog-Sothoth: Umr at'Tawil, The Most Ancient and Prolonged of Life, who presides in a trans-dimensional hall inhabited by beings known only as the Ancient Ones. Umr at'Tawil, a largely benign entity, tests Carter and finds him worthy of passing beyond the ultimate gate, where the human experiences the final revelation and apprehends Yog-Sothoth's true form...

> *It was an All-in-One and One-in-All of limitless being and self - not merely a thing of one Space-Time continuum, but allied to the ultimate animating essence of existence's whole unbounded sweep - the last, utter sweep which has no confines and which outreaches fancy and mathematics alike.*

The ultimate animating essence of existence's whole unbounded sweep. Only that? Lovecraft could certainly never be accused of thinking small![2] And what's more, Carter learns that he himself (and indeed, all creative and/or sorcerous types throughout the aforementioned unbounded sweep) are facets of the great beast that is Yog-Sothoth (now resembling nothing so much as the recumbent Tao of the eastern mystics), glints of light reflecting off its scintillating surface and refracting into the depths of Time, Space, and physical manifestation. Here, Yog-Sothoth reveals itself to be a Platonic ideal, an archetypal being, "outreaching fancy and mathematics alike". *The Prolonged of Life,* for it is Life itself. From this revelation, we may coin the following maxim...

---

1   That old chestnut.

2   Although evidence (from both the story itself and the scholarship surrounding it) would suggest that this grand conceptual construct is better laid at the far more mystically-minded Hoffman Price's door.

All Things are Yog-Sothoth
but some Things are more Yog-Sothoth than others

We are, all of us (and by "all of us" I will boldly turn that Silver Key and reference *every possible manifestation of life and consciousness*) extrusions into this dimension of Yog-Sothoth. Infinitesimal cross-sections of its unthinkable bulk. Lower-order slices of an archetypal Great Being. From this prime Great Old One are all other Old Ones (and Lesser Old Ones, and the uncountable species and beings of the Universe) derived. If Nyarlathotep is the Soul and Mind of the Great Old Ones (a manifestation of the essence of "Meaning"), and Shub-Niggurath the Fertility and Fecundity of them, then Yog-Sothoth is their (and by extension, our) Primal Ground of Being, the quantum potential of All. All are indeed One in Yog-Sothoth, and this *literally* so, though our separate incarnations would suggest otherwise, after the manner of illusions.

Lovecraft, in another letter to his correspondent, acolyte, and friend August Derleth, would claim that Yog-Sothoth was fast becoming an "immature conception" for him, but I contend that this is due more to Lovecraft's own low level of spiritual development (and childish predilection for demonization of things he did not understand) than to any inherent immaturity of the idea of Yog-Sothoth itself. For as a concept, Yog-Sothoth is, yes, serene. Serene and primal.

And if All are One in Yog-Sothoth, then it follows that All are, in some way, Yog-Sothoth. Each of us is a Gate and a Guardian and a Key. The noted British occultist Phillip Hine has spoken of Yog-Sothoth as an experiential boundary state[1], a moment in Time which is entered into that borders on the psychic domain of the Great Old Ones, and this is something with which I concur, with the following proviso: the moment is an eternal one, a door in the desert, and no matter on which side of that door we find ourselves, we are already entered, for we are that door.

For the R'lyehian, it only remains to realize it, to turn the Key and open to ourselves in all our multi-faceted, frothing horror. To walk with Yog-Sothoth is akin to dreaming with Cthulhu: each action is a cultivation of the Black Gnosis, though the latter is necessarily a more personal entryway into that sublime state.

---

1 *The Pseudonomicon*, New Falcon Publications, 2004. First published in a very limited edition in 1994.

Telling the Audient Void:
the Voice of Nyarlathotep

Pity Nyarlathotep.

If there is a voice which accompanies the background radiation of the Universe, a howling between the worlds, then surely that voice belongs to the Crawling Chaos. If there is a keening of despair laced between the pandaemoniac warblings of Azathoth's accompanying flautists, then certainly it must be emitted from the ever-black throat of the Mighty Messenger as he paces in the cosmic wings. For in a creation essentially devoid of meaning, a reality where one of the first principles of manifestation is arbitrary chaos, where communication between entities across all scales of incarnation is largely a fluke of random and necessarily poor internal dictionaries sometimes matching, what creature or deity has more reason for anguish and more capacity for cruelty than Nyarlathotep?

Yes, pity Nyarlathotep, for his is the burden of cobbling together what small meaning can be had from existence, and his the curse of knowing, even as he labours across Time and Space in his Million Forms[1], that whatever he builds is destined to be dust and less than dust, and that he himself is the destroyer of all he creates.

Meaning flares brightly in his skilled, ancient, anguished hands. Meaning (and its pale parasitical phantom, Truth): so chimeric, so fluid, so ultimately empty of itself. This is the mercurial essence that is Nyarlathotep's special province, and his deft handling of it is the result of unknowable aeons of exposure to its particular quicksilver radiation. It flares to brightness at his lightest touch. The briefest of flashes, illuminating and dancing about the heads of conscious entities for a decaying moment before giving way to the

---

1   In other chapters, I spend some words on descriptions of the Great Old Ones. Not so here: Nyarlathotep's avatars are so myriad and multi-form (as befits a being that *is* the essence of Communication) that to do so would fill several larger books, and (as befits a being that *is* the essence of the meaningless-ness at the heart of Communication) still amount to nothing.

shadow of non-existence that rests behind it, ceding power to Those Who Wait Behind the Light.

He is *their* servant. Nyarlathotep is both Messenger and Soul of the Outer Gods, and of the Great Old Ones... and he is more than that, even. He is the flow of light and energy between the stars, the chittering of data through systems of information collection and correlation, the transfer of pulsing chemical packets between cellular walls. Nyarlathotep is electricity and fire, a bolt of summer lightning that leaves the night all the blacker once it has gone to ground.

He is their servant, their Soul and Voice; his service is eternal, his tongue never still. Any wonder that Nyarlathotep is portrayed as capricious, cruel, a haughty trickster-figure more given to destruction than delight? His lessons are terrible, his motives always suspect, and the depth of his dementia is unplumbed. Dementia? As opposed to the Madness of the Black Gnosis which his fellow gods enjoy and embody? Oh yes. Dementia, indeed, for it is his lot, as it is ours, to pre-suppose an order to the chaos, to seek pattern and when it cannot be found (for it *is not there*, not really), to impose it with desperate and furious force. Of course Nyarlathotep suffers dementia, of a kind and scale which we dare not imagine. He cannot simply rest in the Black Gnosis as do the others, he must constantly sift through its contents, rearranging, combining, coaxing it into some semblance of sense, before finally crushing it to dust between his frustrated fingers.

To a beast, the Great Old Ones sleep, dreaming in death... all save for Nyarlathotep, their hungry, wandering ghost. Nyarlathotep is awake. Awake and roaming across the lands and cities of men[1], awake and unable to sleep. A god on permanent haunt through the universe of light, his three-lobed burning eye illuminating all things in the moment before it burns to ash beneath his gaze. Pity Nyarlathotep, for in a very real way, he is the exemplar of our human condition, if not its saviour.

If Yog-Sothoth is the fractured and shifting Primal Ground of Being, and his paramour Shub-Niggurath the forward thrust of the Being into Time, then Nyarlathotep is the story of that so-called progress, the meaning of it, and the communication of that story between its apparently separate elements. Nyarlathotep is a story, *the Story that eats itself*: the original Ouroborous, the snake wrapped round the Tree of Life and winding through to the reverse of that same Tree. Oh, Daathian monstrosity! Is it any wonder that so many of his Million Forms are devourers? Great faceless maws that consume and howl? He is the Mythos itself, given a multitude of forms,

---

1   And here I use the term "men" as a catch-all term for all conscious entities, on all worlds and planes.

active, easily and often tragically encountered by those who would follow the R'lyehian path.

How easily? An experiment: the next time you meet a pre-verbal infant child, watch it closely, particularly if this meeting occurs in a group setting. Put a baby in a room full of adults making what is, to the baby, meaningless gibberish, and that baby will pre-suppose those noises have meaning and then (and here is the key point, the key thing to watch for, if you've the eyes to see it) that baby will invent the idea of language out of whole cloth! Further, it will then learn to communicate in that language, which is, at the end of the day, nothing more than a rather limited set of primate mouth noises. It will construct lexical categories and subject/verb agreements and a host of other syntactical rules. It will do this out of thin air and it will do it without even having a language to think these thoughts in.

Watch the infant closely. Take a moment to look it in the eye. If your tongue does not cleave to the roof of your mouth with the import of it, speak to the child, and maybe you will catch the flash of Nyarlathotep as he manifests, briefly (oh, so painfully briefly!) in the black depths of the pupil. It is a sight to both marvel and shudder at.

And of course, Nyarlathotep manifests in all communications[1]: he is Messenger and Message, the ultimate Medium[2]. He is manifesting now, as these words are laid across the dim glow of my laptop screen, and he will manifest again when they are read on page or tablet, and we small humans that serve as the base matter for this manifestation will nod our heads and marvel and think ourselves momentarily wise. "Ah!" we will say. "We understand!"[3] But we understand nothing, for there is nothing to understand.

---

1 Though he is no mere Hermes, no bright wing-footed courier.

2 We begin to see now the deep connections between the Great Trinity of Yog-Sothoth, Shub-Niggurath, and Nyarlathotep: all are representatives of their respective force, and the means by which it is active, and the subject of its action. Only in Nyarlathotep do we find a conscious resistance to this role, a resistance which creates a dynamic tension that pushes him into greater efforts and greater destruction.

3 I'm saying it now. In my arrogance (which is a mirror of Nyarlathotep's own haughty mein, his resistance against the inevitable) I imagine that this effort of mine, this *book*, is somehow a sensible thing, that it can be understood. Notice how often I write the words "of course", "naturally", and other pompous assurances. Amazing! At the same time, I know and despair (which is a mirror of Nyarlathotep's own anguish) that it is nothing: a collection of idealized mists, a conceptual vapour condensing on the surface of my extremely limited consciousness and given brief expression in physical or electronic form, with the possibility of some miniscule

Human faith and human logic and sciences balk at this. Surely, the more we know, the more meaning is created? With increasing levels of knowledge and denser connectivity between those areas of knowledge, surely our ignorance will be lessened? We forget, conveniently, that the brighter the bonfire, the more darkness it reveals to our eyes. Nyarlathotep is both that bonfire and the Outer Dark it reveals. Mankind, under the guiding hand of Nyarlathotep, will one day correlate all the contents of his knowledge: revelation and madness, that divine Madness which *is* the Black Gnosis, will result.

The R'lyehian, in her efforts to plunge to the center of the Black Gnosis, does her best to make peace with this beautiful thing that awaits us all. The stars will come right. The Great Old Ones will stir, and awaken, and arise...

And Nyarlathotep, their Mighty Messenger, their brother and their Soul, will be gathered back into their bosom, to fall mute and cease his labours. Having freed the universe from the shackles of meaning (through sheer *overuse*) he will, finally, sleep.

---

viral continuity into a future peopled by minds with similar limits.

From this we know, or can at least intuit, that the Psalmist of the Old Testament was perhaps speaking of darker gods than Yahweh when he wrote (with the pen of despair upon the walls of his heart, firstly, before ever putting ink to paper) that all is vanity and a striving after wind, and that there is nothing new under the stars. At least, not until they are right once again, and then? Then all bets are off, I imagine.

But I only imagine. I dream. I am R'lyehian; of course I only dream.

Of *course*.

The Conqueror Womb:
Parsing Shub-Niggurath

At the time of this writing[1], my wife and I are expecting the arrival of our second child, a girl. We are, as we were with our firstborn, naturally excited about the prospect of meeting this new being, this freshly-minted consciousness, and look forward to sharing in her growing awareness of herself and the world.

We are also, as thinking humans and R'lyehians, appropriately *appalled* by the prospect, and particularly the nature and manner of her arrival into our lives. Common wisdom claims the birth of a child as a small, everyday miracle, but too few individuals ever really explore the awesome and terrifying implications of sexuality, breeding, and birth against the vast background tapestry of Time and Space. But this we must do, to arrive at an appreciation of the ultimate temporal insurgency and animating essence of Shub-Niggurath: the Prime Mover in the Ooze, Mother of Abominations, Fractal Felitrix of Fecundity.

Our daughter is more active than our son was. Not to put too fine a point on it: she's a kicker. A kicker at the walls of her rapidly contracting universe. She is also, with only eight weeks to go, still in a breech position, which means her kicks tend to land with brutal precision on the inside of her mother's cervix...

"Goddamnit! I swear she's going to punch a hole right out of me," said my wife recently, after a particularly vigorous internal assault.

"She wants to get started," I replied.

Of course, that's not actually the case: babies *in utero* have no conceptual tools or structures with which to create such a conscious desire or drive in themselves. Kicks, in this case, are merely kicks. Nevertheless, there is something of truth in the statement, for it cannot be denied that, as far as the career of Life itself is concerned, we are nothing *but* drive: a constant,

---

1   Our daughter, Meridian, was born at 6:28pm, October 2, 2013. This book is dedicated to her.

frantic, multi-limbed *pushing* forward into the stuff of Time, and a concurrent dominance of Space and progressively higher dimensions.

From the first free-floating amoebas, directionless and adrift in ancient dimly-lit seas, to the precision-guided humans describing perfect parabolas miles above our planet at this very second, the goal of Life has always been to consume the past in a holocaust of present forms, each a potential beachhead on the future, a probe into the Possible. We are, each of us, the leading edge of every iteration of the genetic code that came before us, down through unthinkable eons of aunts and apes, arcteryx and annelid. We are, each of us, the very tip of a branch on the Tree of Life.

And that Tree, that grasping, thrusting, engulfing storm of Being, that Tree *is* Shub-Niggurath, the Black Goat of the Woods[1] with A Thousand Young.

"Did you know that right now, I'm not only carrying our daughter, but technically our grandchildren as well?" My wife loves her research. "All her eggs are present within her already."

"That's if we win the evolutionary lottery, and our offspring breed successfully. We have *potential* grandchildren at this moment. Well, half our potential grandchildren, anyway." I took a moment to breathe, to feel the ridiculous gravity of the future pull at my core. "Such extravagance," I muttered. "So many eggs in you... how many, actually?"

"Well, at this moment, whatever I've got left myself, so, maybe just under 300,000." she answered. "She's got around two million. There's a lot of egg cell die-off between birth and puberty."

"Still. More than anyone would ever need in a thousand lifetimes. And that's nothing in comparison to the horde of swimmers present in each humble little spurt of my ejaculate. Twenty million or more. Twenty *million*. My seed, over my lifetime, is in the..." I found myself momentarily at a loss, boggling at the scale of it all. "Dagon's Teeth, what's the number grouping that's higher than billions?"

"Trillions."

"*Trillions*. It's in the trillions. Only *two* of which have resulted in actual fresh humans. The extravagance! Madness!"

---

1 The tale is told of the armies of the Roman Empire as they advanced into the Germanic territories, and of the moment when they first arrived at the edge of the Black Forest, only to shrink back in superstitious retreat at the sheer size, scale, and massed numbers of the trees. Any large, ancient wood will have this affect on the sensitive, for it is a picture of Time made vegetable, conquered and choked by life. The forest is the domain of Shub-Niggurath.

Truly, Shub-Niggurath is the Conqueror Womb. All shall fall, all *are* falling, before her miscegenetic might, her inexhaustible infinite armies of mingling microscopic code. For what is Life but a swarm of information expressed in flesh over the entirety of Time? If we were to somehow view the career of Life in a time-lapsed fashion, that is what we would see: a swarm of forms, a frothing shoggoth-wave of embodied information, a wave the leading edge of which we are poised upon, always and in all ways.

Shub-Niggurath, to borrow a phrase from Zen, is both the water of Life, the actual matter of it, the flesh and the fury, and the wave, the temporal moving point within the matter. She is Fertility and all that the word implies. If Yog-Sothoth, her paramour, is the extruding force of consciousness and awareness into our dimension(s), then Shub-Niggurath is the provider of the receiving forms for that consciousness. She is the Ultimate Mothering Pot.

These forms, whether of flesh, silicon, plasma, or spirit, share one thing in common with their Source: hunger. Not for nothing is Shub-Niggurath portrayed in much of the Mythos-related fiction as a deity of vast appetite, for she is the embodiment of the First Rule of the Universe: Everybody Hungry. This hunger manifests in various ways: for food, territory, information, experience. All these things must be consumed, in whole or in part, and all to feed the First Hunger itself: the hunger for Time, for the Future, a hunger that can only be sated through sex and procreation.

Time is often characterized as a consuming fire in which all things burn. Time the Thief. Time and its grim, chalky cheerleader Death: two heads of the tag-teaming Conqueror Worm. Shub-Niggurath, the Conqueror Womb, shows us that the opposite is true: we (that is to say *Life*) are that which consumes Time. We are the hungry ghosts, moving from body to body, and beyond bodies into epigenetic technologies and airy Platonic idea-forms, and we pass the seconds and minutes and eons through the needle-narrow throats of our endless iterations. We are not the victims of Time. Time is our food, we take from it what we need, and once we have consumed it, it becomes fixed in the past, immovable and essentially dead.

Another view, one relating to the Dark Young of Shub-Niggurath: the Future is always dark, which is to say formless and unknown. To consume Time, to feed the Future through the choke-point of consciousness and being, of manifestation, is to expose it to the illumination of the Present, a brightness which calcifies and stiffens it. The Dark Young of Shub-Niggurath, then, are the forms of Life yet to be manifested, permanent residents of that threshold state just beyond the Now. Recall the description, given by the sometime Mythos-author Robert Bloch in his classic story *Notebook Found in a Deserted House*...

Something black in the road, something that wasn't a tree. Something big and black and ropy, just squatting there, waiting, with ropy arms squirming and reaching ... it was the black thing of my dreams - that black, ropy, slime jelly tree-thing out of the woods. It crawled up and it flowed up on its hoofs and mouths and snaky arms.

What is this image of a single Dark Young, if it is not a composite form of the shifting, viscous flesh of genetic possibility? Of some future chimeric proto-manifestation of a life force not yet locked down into a single form? Mouths and ropes and snakes and hoofs and trees, a being (or myriad beings!) vibrating with quantum uncertainty at every point of intersection with the moment that is to come, the one just after this one! The Dark Young of Shub-Niggurath: agents of the ultimate insurgency.

But why is such an insurgency necessary? Why must Time be consumed, processed, shat out? All things move toward their end: Time, though the thing *through* which all things move, is itself no exception to this cosmic law, and so we see the goal of the Great Old Ones brought closer to fruition by the activities of Life at the behest of the Mother, the Conqueror Womb...

*That is not dead, which can eternal lie
and with strange aeons, even Death may die*

Yog-Sothoth knows the Gates and is the Key to them; Shub-Niggurath is the pressing of the flesh against those Gates, and when the Great Old Ones awaken and return to their full consciousness and might, that which bursts through will be her spawn. Shub-Niggurath devours Time to hasten the moment of their return, or, to be rather more crude about it, Shub-Niggurath fucks Time to death.

The R'lyehian, knowing this, and knowing the method whereby this devouring is accomplished, has her answer to the nihilist and the anti-natalist. The latter claims that, given the cruelty and suffering inherent to incarnating in this world, the worst cruelty a sentient being can commit is being party to the creation of yet another sentient being.

This view supposes that survival-in-the-flesh somehow means survival-of-the-individual. The R'lyehian knows there is no such thing. The R'lyehian knows that "the individual" is a momentary condensation of consciousness (itself an extrusion of Yog-Sothoth) on the shifting surface of flesh and form, and any pain or joy "the individual" experiences is likewise momentary.

Just as we are all Yog-Sothoth, so, too, are we the Dark Young of Shub-Niggurath: we are mind and consciousness, and the base matter that houses consciousness for brief moments, birthing and dying in our unguessable numbers, and all of it surging towards the point when Time (exhausted, devoured, and unable to hold its shape against the onslaught of the First Hunger) finally shatters, ending the cycle. At that point, the stars will come right.

As the Buddhists affirm, only in Time is suffering possible. Is not its destruction the awesome work of gods? Is it not the ultimate Great Work, performed by Ones no less Great?

To Shub-Niggurath, then, Primal Kali, Annihilating Dark Mother, Black Goat of the Woods with a Thousand Young, the R'lyehian offers praise and, so far as they are able, abundance[1].

---

1 see the chapter *The Unbearable Strangeness of Being: Sex and the R'lyehian*

A Certain Sort of Men:
Dagon & the Deep One Aesthetic

The R'lyehian is a transitional creature, a thing of the shoreline and the spaces between states of Being. She is human in body and to a lesser extent in mind, but she holds within herself so much void, so many honeycombed surfaces that define the hollow spaces, surfaces which the Black Gnosis may adhere itself to, that to speak of her as a hybrid thing is more than correct.

The R'lyehian lives and creates in multiple worlds simultaneously, and does so with relative ease. He transitions between them as well, constantly. For this reason, an examination of the esoteric aspects of the Deep Ones, who are in many ways a kind of evolutionary precursor to the R'lyehian, will be beneficial, and of course there can be no discussion of the Deep Ones, those archaic leapers-between-the-worlds, without a discussion of their lord and King of the Voltiguers, Father Dagon.

Dagon's place in our pantheon here is a unique one, for unlike his fellows, his first appearance as a god on this planet predates his inclusion in Lovecraft's Mythos: Dagon was, originally[1], a god of the Phoenicians, a being who rose from the depths of the sea to bring technology, the arts, agriculture and writing to the early Aegean and Mesopotamia. In this guise, and often under the name Oannes, he is depicted as a protean humanoid figure with prominent fishy *accoutrements*, which may be construed as either ceremonial garb or, in the more perplexing (to non-R'lyehian minds) representations, parts of his actual body.

Even in this early form, the lineaments of the Great Old One we know now are present, though blurred by primitive human understanding. Dagon here is amphibious, a being of many worlds, imparting knowledge and advanced technologies on ignorant surface-dwellers in return for worship and, one can only assume, something in the nature of sacrifice, though this is never explicitly stated.

---

1 "Originally", at least, as far as historical human cultures are concerned.

Naturally, the mind jumps to the obvious sacrificial choices: blood and lives, the virginity of maidens, and so on. Though such offerings never really go out of style, as R'lyehians we must entertain the notion that Father Dagon (at least in this ancient incarnation) had something else in mind. Why gift air-breathing apes, barely out of their caves in the hills, with culture, arts, progress, *thinking*? There is nothing in this life that is not, somehow, contractual, and dealings with gods are certainly not exempt from this rule. *What does the deity gain?* This is the question that must be asked.

Dagon is the King of the Voltigeurs, the Prime Leaper Between the Worlds. All things batrachian are under his gaze; his totem is the frog, which in one moment rests in utter stillness on lily pad or stone and in the next is gone from sight, leaving only ripples and after-images, so swift is its spring. What would such a being, itself progenitor to an entire race of like-yet-lesser beings, the Deep Ones, need of endowing humans with power and agency?

Clearly, Dagon is a god who, Prometheus-like, wants to get us up to speed. But to what end? The goal of such an action is always to bring to the younger species some form of parity with the gods. And parity with the gods can only be achieved through the shattering of the barriers between the mundane and the spiritual.

The Great Old Ones are changeless: thousands of years later, in Lovecraft's short tale *Dagon,* we see the same drives at work.

A nameless protagonist writes of the events which have driven him to insanity. Worse things happen at sea, as the saying goes, and he finds himself stranded on a vast muck-encrusted island only recently emerged from the cold depths, where he encounters Father Dagon in a penultimate scene of primal might and moonlit terror. The god breaks the surface of immemorial ocean to retrieve from the island's crags an eidolon: a monolith of staggering proportions, engraved with scenes both beautiful and horrible. Father Dagon embraces the stone before sinking with it back into the ebon seeps. Divinely inspired Madness falls like a hammer upon the protagonist; the merest glimpse of Dagon's form is enough to plunge him into the Black Gnosis.

He is unregenerate, though, and cannot conceive of his experience as anything other than direst horror, even after his escape from that swiftly sinking land mass and his eventual rescue. He has seen a Great Old One, and lived to tell. The interesting aspect of the story comes towards the end, as the protagonist withers beneath the weight of his knowledge, alone in a garret, jacked up on morphine, desiring only forgetfulness or death. The former cannot happen and we are given to understand that the latter is guaranteed. In a classic piece of italicized Lovecraftian climax, as he cringes from the sound of "some immense slippery body lumbering against" the door, he writes his final words: *God, that hand! The window! The window!*

On the face of it, we are to assume that the narrator has met his end. Certainly that was Lovecraft's intention: he *was* crafting a horror story, after all. But then, from a spiritual perspective, it's equally certain that a god has sought out a man. A higher order being has extended a portion of itself towards a lower order one. The implications are staggering: Father Dagon (or at the very least one of his Deep One representatives) has gone so far as to *pay a personal visit to the very door of a man.*

One cannot help but picture the hokey inspirational artwork of the Christians: Jesus knocking upon a door in the middle of the night, lamp in hand. With the Dagon/Deep One/human interaction, we are perhaps too quick to assume that this visit is paid solely to serve out a death sentence. Might it not also be in an effort to save? An evangelism of the Deep? Cold, wet, wise webbed hands searching out the dry and foolish palms of angry apes breathing their thin, mournful airs?[1]

---

1   Though this comparison may be troublesome, a number of interesting (and indeed, fairly obvious) corollaries can be made between various figures in the Gospels and the Great Old Ones, between the Christian faith and that of the R'lyehian. For instance, Cthulhu, dead but dreaming and rising at the appointed time in the cycle of eternity, "when the stars are once again right", to free the Universe from the stagnant grip of rationality, may be seen to correspond with the Christ figure, a Redeemer who unites all under a new heavens and upon a new earth. And if that is so, then may Dagon also correspond to John the Baptist, who prepared the way for the Christ by permeating the wall between Judaism and the coming new faith using the sacrament of baptismal submergence? Dagon performs a similar function, dissolving the barriers between whole worlds of thought and being.

Certainly, the *piscis sofia* of early Gnostic Christian thought must factor into our discussion. Fishers of men... or fish-men? Either way, we find ourselves in the water. One need only extend the curves of the "Christian fish" symbol to arrive at a potent glyph diagramming the overlapping of two higher-order realities; something most bumper-sticker Christians are completely ignorant of. Indeed, early Christianity bears little resemblance to the relatively bright and chipper, if blinkered, religion we see around us today. The apocrypha blister with Archons and spheres, qliphotic shells and cosmos-spanning angelic wars, riddles dripping from the slack lips of idiotic blind creator-gods.

In the end, it is only the Gnosis which is important, that clarifying pure awareness of our true place in the universe, the knowledge of the deep things of the Deep Ones, howsoever it may be approached.

Dagon leaps between worlds, has *seen* many worlds. He knows their wonders and glories, their benefits, their follies. When he reaches out to us, echoing the greater, deeper Call of his own master, Cthulhu, who are we to refuse that union?

And yet that is what occurred, and on a species-wide scale. In Dagon's early form, that of Oannes, this personal attention was extended to the human species. Solidarity, and parity, was the core motivation at work. A solidarity which, given our propensity for delusion and ungratefulness, likely (if history is to be trusted) did not result in the kind of union Dagon sought.

So we are left, then, with a degenerate form of union, which Lovecraft explicated in the next tale he wrote concerning the croaking submarine followers of Father Dagon, *The Shadow Over Innsmouth*.

In that tale, the narrator, one Robert Olmstead, learns of the slow infiltration and degradation of the titular town, as certain of its leaders have made pact with a colony of Deep Ones off the coast. Sacrifice is implied, and cross-breeding with the inhabitants of "Devil's Reef" is a key element of the pact. In return, wealth is bestowed upon the town: strange golden artifacts, sceptres and tiaras and ceremonial tools[1], and an increase in the bounty from fishing. Immortality, as well, for those residents fortunate enough to experience the genetic change that comes from the inter-species coupling: beyond and below the surface grotesqueries of the "Innsmouth look" is a retro-evolutionary shift, from human to full Deep One, and an eventual return to the sea, to the wondrous, gloried depths and phosphorescent halls

---

1 In the tale, our batrachian ancestors ("a certain sort of men", indeed: brothers from a far distant other mother *and* father) are, in fact, Makers of a very high order. Though Lovecraft predictably presents them as monsters, in almost the next breath he contradicts this by stating that their cities are vast and beautiful, their technologies wondrous beyond understanding, and their mastery of magic and ultra-telluric sorceries near-total. Below the waves, their rule (with Father Dagon at their head) is complete.

This Deep One "Maker" aesthetic can and should be mapped onto the early stages of R'lyehian spiritual development. Before the Black Gnosis takes hold of consciousness, it is helpful to anticipate and hasten its arrival through deep involvement with the arts: sculpture, painting, writing, music and so on. The magical act of creation, of the type that comes as a result of one-pointed awareness, is extremely helpful in triggering entry into the Black Gnosis. The R'lyehian who weighs down her psyche with such talismans crafted with her own hands and skill (talismans which have a presence both in mundane reality and the oneiric realms) sinks into the nighted depths of R'lyeh that much faster. See the chapter *The Wisdom in the Clay* for more discussion on the R'lyehian and the arts.

of Y'ha-nthlei. These are the rewards, and the costs, of membership in the Esoteric Order of Dagon.

The taint of the cross-breeding, the Innsmouth look, is a key issue here, for the visibility and utter strangeness of the physical mutations that occur with Deep One contact make the town a target of dark rumour, rising suspicion, and finally a full attack by Federal authorities. In the depths off Devil Reef, naval submarines rain down destruction upon Y'ha-nthlei while the town above is raided and burned. The Deep Ones survive, for they always have, but their surface paramours and worshipers fare poorly, meeting incarceration or death. Hints are made that the Deep Ones will rise again, in another attempt at infiltration with an insurgency against the human world, and on a larger scale, but one immediately wonders how such a thing could happen, considering the clear failure of the Innsmouth experiment[1].

Olmstead (in a climax that is, again, meant to chill the unregenerate reader even as it offers up a vision of redemption and transcendence to the one whose eyes are open) learns of his own matrilineal kinship with the lords of Y'ha-nthlei and closes the account with his plans to rescue from an insane asylum a similarly tainted cousin before stepping into the waves and vanishing from the human world...

> *We shall swim out to that brooding reef in the sea and dive down through black abysses to Cyclopean and many-columned Y'ha-nthlei, and in that lair of the Deep Ones we shall dwell amidst wonder and glory forever.*

Which is all very well and good, and clearly (for Olmstead) a consummation devoutly to be wished, but for the R'lyehian it smacks of retreat. To borrow from Christian terminology again, this final dive is akin to hiding ones light beneath a bushel. What use is it to bask in submarine glories if that glory cannot be manifested somehow on the surface? What good a dive to depths of wonder if that wonder is still faintly illuminated by the light of the rational sun? Yes, there is much to learn from an exploration of the Deep Down, and many reasons to stay there once arrived, but it is a zone of the unconscious ocean that supports a kind of life that cannot rise to the surface

---

1   In a telling sentence, this plan even appears to be contingent on, of all things, *mood*, or at least record-keeping skills: "For the present they would rest; but some day, *if they remembered*, they would rise again for the tribute Great Cthulhu craved." *The Shadow Over Innsmouth*, H. P. Lovecraft (italics mine)

without becoming distorted with the change in pressure, a life that is not truly amphibious. Attempt the land again after too long in Y'ha-nthlei and risk a kind of psychic Bends that warps the consciousness in, yes, interesting ways, but also *telling* ways that brand the surfacer immediately as Outsider.

So, though congress and commerce with the Deep Ones may result in great and unusual wealth, and though homage must be paid to Father Dagon as the exemplar and prophet of Cthulhu, the R'lyehian at the same time acknowledges their limitations. Their gnosis is incomplete; glorious, but stunted. They are unable to camouflage themselves and move among men, and so will always be spotted, ostracized, hounded. They wear the taint of their weirdness on their skin and dress themselves in antique oddments that mark them for what they are: a regressive, retrograde species belonging more to the past ages of earth than the future. The Deep Ones, magnificent and strange as they are, are all about sating their needs and then sinking below the waves once more[1].

The R'lyehian, on the other webbed hand, is about *rising*. The R'lyehian honours the ancient contract of Dagon and seeks true parity with him, with a view to destroying the barriers between his world and ours, to making the stars come right again. For R'lyeh to rise in every human heart, every human heart must be won by the Great Old Ones, and this *cannot* happen when the human body is repulsed by the Innsmouth look, or when the human mind is tainted with the incomplete gnosis of shiny gold trinkets and point-less miscegenation.

The leap between worlds *must* be instantaneous and complete, as Dagon desires for us, if we are to serve his master, Cthulhu, in the way it deserves. If we are to attain the Black Gnosis. The R'lyehian strives to be a *true* amphibian, equally at home on the streets as he is in the deeps. He does not shamble or flop loathsomely, hiding his form beneath poorly fitting clothes, and neither does he flail ineffectively in the sea like a waterlogged ape, gasping for breath with half-formed gills.

The Deep One is of the past. The human is of the present.

The R'lyehian is of the future.

---

1 Whole Deep One populations, for instance, can be found on a yearly migratory circuit through various conventions (or "cons", both Lovecraftian and otherwise) held across many nations. The wares and *very* specialized knowledge displayed at these gatherings can be staggering and enticing, but the R'lyehian knows the folly of being drawn in to these intricate yet shallow mazes, mazes which merely ape the non-Euclidean lacework of the lowliest suburb of the Dreaming City.

On Cthulhu

Of all the cosmically potent and trans-temporal entities that comprise the incomprehensible pantheon of the Great Old Ones, there is one that merits special attention by any scholar/practitioner of R'lyehian spirituality. One being, whom, above all others, is deserving of study, respect, midnight thoughts, worship, and supplication. It is, of course, the Prime R'lyehian, the Highest of the High Priests of the Great Old Ones, the Lord of Dreams and Secret Chief of Those Who Wait Behind the Light. The Sleeping Serpent. The Fount of Madness. Primal Source of the Black Gnosis. The Big C...

Cthulhu.

"Let that roll around on your tongue for a bit, mammal. Mangled, yet? It should be! For no human vocal apparatus could possibly produce the true sound of... "

You're forgiven for suppressing a yawn just there. Because that's the kind of thing you'd hear in the sort of geek-centric circles where things such as the correct pronunciation of that Name are deemed important; a sad touchstone for any number of useless arguments and chest-puffings. The Name has been variously transcribed as Tulu, Clulu, Cthulu, C'thulhu, Cighulu, Q'thulu, K'tulu, Kthulhut, Kutunluu, Ktulu, Cuitiliú, and Thu Thu. Lovecraft himself was known to on occasion (and not without some variation between instances) instruct his correspondents thusly...

> *... The first syllable is pronounced gutturally and very thickly. The* u *is about like that in full; and the first syllable is not unlike* klul *in sound, hence the* h *represents the guttural thickness...*[1]

---

1   H. P. Lovecraft, *Selected Letters V*, pp. 10-11

Here, *Cthulhu* is rendered less as an articulate sound and more as a kind of glottal grunt carried with difficulty on the back of a hacking cough, trailing off with a half-hearted expulsion of whatever air remains in the lungs. Hardly an impressive vocalization.

The most common pronunciation by far, though, is kuh-THOO-loo. This sound (which could be argued is the obvious way to say it; I myself have heard complete newcomers to the Name voice it so) was made popular by Sandy Peterson, originator of the *Call of Cthulhu* role-playing game, an entertainment franchise which has enjoyed considerable longevity since its creation in 1981, and some claim has been responsible for the current resurgence of interest, here in the 21st Century, for all things related to the Mythos.

Which is all very well and good, since none of these are correct, naturally.

For how can the unpronounceable ever be pronounced? The unnameable thing named? And since there is no possible way to say it, then all ways of saying it are valid, if flawed. The Name, Cthulhu, is merely a place holder, and not a very good one at that, for the active principle of Dreaming and Madness that lies behind the Name. The Name is the Mask that hides the Reality. Even if some talented sorcerer-linguist managed, with extensive surgery to her vocal equipment and practice, to somehow produce the Name as it *truly* sounds, even *that* attempt would fail, for the true pronunciation of the Name goes far deeper, plunging like a fiery meteor into a sea of blood. Deep, deep into the source of the Black Gnosis.

As an example, speak your own name: that small collection of vowels and consonants pinned to your soul at birth, those words, not chosen by you (at least, not consciously, leaving aside for the moment the notion of a pre-life, a before-world where such choices may be pondered), which serve as the anchor for your identity in this world. Do others share your name? Unless yours is utterly unique (a condition that either speaks to the creativity or cruelty, or both, of your parents), then yes, there are other beings out there that carry it, some in whole and most in part. You all pronounce it similarly, you *Daves* and *Sandras* and *Mustaphas*, yet each of you carry an entire complex of history, emotion, ideas about the self, and relationship with that name, a complex that is particular to you and may be shared, if only in an imperfect fashion, with your associates and those close to you. Your name is spoken, hundreds of thousands of times a day, but only *you* may say it and know it for yours.

Similarly, only Cthulhu itself could say the Name correctly, and mean it, and most importantly, embody it. For Cthulhu *is* Madness. Cthulhu *is* the Black Gnosis, and many other things and qualities which the dedicated R'lyehian aspires to, besides. When the stars are right, Cthulhu speaks its

Name, which is also its Call, and we who have made of our minds suburbs of the great city of R'lyeh hear it. We hear it, snaking through the twisted streets and warped alleyways we have carved in our own heads. The Name moves like sentient smoke through a consciousness made R'lyehian. We hear it, and breathe it in, and allow it to enter us in unfathomable ways, and we know.

We know Cthulhu and experience the Black Gnosis, and though we may never speak of it properly, never cognize its dark blessing in any way that could be called understandable, we may approach it, and the qualities of Cthulhu which it carries, by speaking first of the form of Great Cthulhu.

It is significant that of all the alien monster-gods that Lovecraft populated his fledgling Mythos with, Cthulhu is the most humanoid[1]. Its form is plastic and loathsome and yet it follows certain rudimentary anthropoid outlines. Lovecraft perceived it as a hideous amalgam of cephalopod, dragon and man. Imagine a human frame, flabby, grotesque, with a distended abdomen bloated from long centuries of unknowable digestive processes, the hands and feet clawed and strangely muscled. Take this frame and graft to the shoulder blades long, bony wings of shredded tissue. Now place upon the shoulders of the thing an armoured squid, pulpy and writhing: this will serve as the head. Finally, blow the whole abomination up until it is the size of a mountain. And then, as any sane imagination would do, sink it deep in a submarine chasm and bind it with signs so that it will not arise to revel in destruction and mayhem...

> *The Thing cannot be described - there is no language for such abysms of shrieking and immemorial lunacy, such eldritch contradictions of all matter, force, and cosmic order. A mountain walked or stumbled. God!"*

— H. P. Lovecraft, *The Call of Cthulhu*

God, indeed. Yet clearly, we have just described it, made relatively decent approximations of Cthulhu's general outline. Having done so, we cannot help but wonder: why *this* form? Why a chimeric merging of man, dragon,

---

1 Dagon notwithstanding. The Voltigeur King is clearly also of anthropoid outline, but, as explained in the previous chapter, that deity and its offspring are of a deeper, primitive time. Dagon and the Deep Ones are symbolic pre-cursors to Cthulhu and the R'lyehian.

and cephalopod? Why, when the other beings of the Mythos are form*less* frothings, or possessing of multiple forms, which is as good as having no form? Azathoth is a withering blight of nuclear chaos residing at the centre of the Universe, attended to by equally shapeless and chaotic lesser forms; Yog Sothoth, the All-In-One and One-In-All, presents as a shimmering congeries of iridescent globes; Shub-Niggurath, the fertility goddess-thing, is a vague, amorphous mass of constantly budding protoplasm; the Crawling Chaos, Nyarlathotep, appears in *millions* of possible avatars. Only in Cthulhu is there a solid form and recognizable attributes, and these strangely derived from the human at that.

Why this distinct shape, Lovecraft? Why any shape at all?

The discerning reader cannot fail to notice the peculiar totemic resonance of the above descriptors. Two arms, two legs, a trunk from which these appendages hang: the kinship with man is obvious. The wings less so, but wings (functional or not) are representative of *flight*, and flight symbolizes ascent, speed, transcendence above and beyond the mundane lower dimensions. The tentacled, cephalopodic head, of course, reminds us of the octopus, one of the most highly intelligent creatures of the sea; adaptable, problem-solving, and with its astonishing capacity for swift colour change and shape-shifting, the creature practically wears its thought processes on its skin. In this way, it may even be telepathic.

Lovecraft's Cthulhu displays all these powers, from dissolving into a green mist when rammed by an ignorant skipper and then reforming after the boats passing, to the ability to navigate through the non-Euclidean geometries of its submarine prison-tomb, to infiltrating the minds of sleeping dreamers. And then, as a symbol, the octopus is obviously a single hub with eight arms radiating outward, a fact not lost on our Pythagorean sensibilities. Here are qualities of sidereal thinking, active assimilation of diverse strands of knowledge, multi-tasking to the *nth* degree, and the ability to embrace multiple realities simultaneously. The cephalopodic head matched to the winged body is a glorious combination of attributes, symbolic of the latent genetic traits of the human animal, traits which are suppressed and stultified by the Apollonian energies of the modern, rational world.

But even this form may be merely a totemic feint. This form is, as already mentioned, *Lovecraft's* Cthulhu. We must not forget that these limbs, these wings, this loathsome flabbiness, these "abysms of shrieking and immemorial lunacy", these are but the clothes that one imaginative human dressed Madness in. These scales and feelers, these prodigious claws: the Mask crafted during all-night, long-hand writing sessions by a single, malnourished, reclusive New England man over the summer of 1926.

The Black Gnosis that is Cthulhu's gift to the R'lyehian practitioner, that *is* Cthulhu, does not reside in the form. It is not the Mask itself, but what it conceals. Granted, a certain slavish devotion to the form has produced any number of fantastic representations: sculptures, paintings, digital renderings that can take the breath away with their "exquisitely artistic workmanship" that is "frightfully suggestive of old and unhallowed cycles of life in which our world and our conceptions have no part," as Lovecraft put it in his story.

But it is that same devotion that leads to the dumbing-down of Cthulhu, to the point where it has become a pop-cultural visual shorthand for ancient malevolence and extreme horror. Even within the previously mentioned geek-centric circles, Great Cthulhu is, at best, little better than a great joke. An excuse to mime a gibbering session. Something to put on a t-shirt, to turn into a plush doll. A target for parody, for satire. At its worst, Cthulhu serves as a tongue-in-cheek object of "worship" for bored atheists and agnostics who can't be bothered to cobble up a smirking deity of their own.

I have seen the results of this dumbing-down first hand. Over the summer of 2011, I took my one-man spoken-word show *The Boy's Own Guide to Sorcery* on a multi-city tour across western Canada. Depending on the crowd, I would, over the course of the performance, touch on some of these points. Not long after the tour, I received an email from an audience member. A younger fellow, he certainly *knew* of Cthulhu, but only from his own exposure to the Pop version: Cthulhu®™. After complaining that the Big C was "not very scary or madness inducing", he went on...

> *And lastly, something I never quite understood. How can Cthulhu be the Platonic ideal of madness and also a giant green thing? Because I'm relatively sane, and I can conceive of a giant green octopus-monster. I'm open-minded to the idea that he is in fact madness, but I definitely don't yet see it.*

It's this erroneous perception of Cthulhu as a "giant green octopus-monster" that has created the tongue-in-cheek culture that surrounds it. In the minds of most, this version of the Lord of Dreams sits comfortably in the realm of the Japanese *kaiju*: titanic beasts that do little more than stomp and eat and cause untold destruction. Granted, Cthulhu's debut in Lovecraft's story was accompanied by imaginative visuals of just that kind of behaviour, visuals so compelling, it's easy to see how its other aspects would be so blocked.

The mind that insists on this interpretation is, frankly, weak. Weak, and much given to adolescent fantasies of revenge and entitlement. Surely, the Great Cthulhu will favour the faithful by, say, eating them first ("A mercy! *Iä, iä! Fhtagn!*" and so on) when it rises from the depths, before moving on to the unregenerate and the non-believers, like some cosmic glutton bellying up to a planet-wide buffet. Always with the *eating*, I've noticed with these ones. The oral fixation of the childish. As if the destruction of the corporeal form was all Cthulhu was good for, or capable of! No. No, it is far more than that...

Consider the other qualities of the Lord of Dreams. Qualities which, when amortized out over the vigintillions of years Great Cthulhu has been in touch with this world, begin to take on greater significance for the true R'lyehian...

Dreaming

This is the premier communication medium between the R'lyehian and the Lord of R'lyeh. In dreams, we navigate strange angles, taste forbidden and monstrous emotions, participate in irrational rituals and experience altered sexualities and modes of being. This is so even in what could (with a straight face or not) be called *normal dreaming*. What a concept! No dream is normal! We become *used* to dreaming, yes, and over time we take it to be a natural thing. Most become so bored with the contents of their nightly visions that they soon forget or ignore the fact that dreaming happens at all.

But it does. It does happen, and in more forms than we can know. Just as there are zones in the ocean, from the neritic through the cold seeps to the benthic, so, too, are there zones of Dream, states of awareness, of dreaming consciousness. Exo-personalities, soul-armours, and meta-tanks of psychic atmosphere are needed in order to survive there; tools that allow the dreamer to sink deep and return intact. In sleep, the mind drops like a stone into pressured, ebon depths.

The rationalists (of whatever stripe) among us will say that dreams are the mere residue of waking cognitive function. That those dreams which can be remembered are the sometimes chaotic, sometimes randomly meaningful froth of a brain untethered to bodily sensation, fizzing by itself in the dark, like some giddy captive of the Mi-Go[1]. These rationalists (bleeding to a man from the constant self-inflicted strokes of Occam's Razor against their

---

1 Lovecraft's "Fungi from Yuggoth": alien insectoid beings fond of brain-napping and cosmic tourism.

ravaged flesh!) would go on to claim that in those nighted depths of dream that permit no recall, there is no life. In this, they are only half-right.

For Cthulhu is there. Dead, but dreaming.

The R'lyehian knows this, because the R'lyehian enters her dreams each night with one goal: to dive, as deeply as possible, beyond the individualistic ephemera of surface dreams, beyond even the twilight realms associated with the diffused common material of the human species. Past and through this detritus she dives, she sinks, into crushing abyssal nothingness, and she does not stop until she feels the stones of R'lyeh manifest beneath her quaking feet.

For the R'lyehian, dreaming is communion. To dream *there*, on the twisting steps of Cthulhu's tomb, is to *be* Cthulhu, to *be* Madness. For the R'lyehian, to wander the warp and weft of the streets of that Eternal City is the purest, terrifying bliss. To linger by the shoggoth middens, to ponder hieroglyphs and graffiti alike, to navigate impossible angles and be swallowed by them, to be spat out changed from what he was before being swallowed, to prostrate himself before Things That Cannot Be, is enlightenment for him. Each contact with R'lyeh and its inhabitant, whether remembered consciously or not, allows the dreamer to bring a scrap of R'lyeh back with them, into the waking world. There is no way to properly cognize or speak about what this surfacing can look like: it is individual to each R'lyehian, utterly private and rarely expressible, and may manifest in the world and in their own consciousness any number of ways.

For me, the signature mode of this surfacing in my own life is the incomprehensible channeled textual artifacts that are produced under trance. Even this, though, is only the most visible condensation of the R'lyehian aesthetic in the world of deeds and ideas. I have left hastily manufactured fetishes on public transport and in hidden places. I have spoken words (some few known to me, most not at all) at various places and certain times, not knowing why, unaware even, until the moment of speaking, that the word was there on my tongue. Signs have been unconsciously drawn in the air with one hand while the other was busy with another, more mundane task; my attention called to the action by those present. I have bled into the sea and gibbered beneath the stars. In these ways, and uncountable others, is R'lyeh raised.

To open oneself to being a conduit for R'lyehian energy, to become a line of circuitry in Cthulhu's matrix of Dreaming Madness, is to find oneself living, with eyes open, in the trans-rational logic and shuddering pleasure of Dream itself.

It is the responsibility, the glory, and the joy of each R'lyehian to dream in this fashion. To dream, to dive, to commune with Madness: this is a grasping of the celestial clockwork and wrenching it, cog by resistant cog, into a more favourable configuration. To dream, asleep and awake, is to make the stars right, within and without.

Raise R'lyeh, one stone at a time.

Waiting

Much is made of Cthulhu's form, Cthulhu's might, Cthulhu's potency and potential for destruction and chaos, for rending a world upon its waking from the dream of Death. Though the R'lyehian looks forward, obviously, towards such a transformation of all that lives and exists, for the remaking of the world in fire and ice and deep, cold waters, she also is aware of the cycles of deep Time in which the Great Old Ones are embedded, and of the supreme quality of patience that is one of the genuine hallmarks of their High Priest, Cthulhu.

It is said that when the stars are *not* right, they cannot live, which is a fine thing to say on the surface of it. A small morsel of hope, perhaps? The musings of the ignorant, most likely. It is said that they are held, dead or dormant, or whatever passes for these states with such beings, imprisoned in the deep places of the Earth, bound Outside our various dimensions and planes and spheres, barred from passing through gates. But are we really to believe that the trans-temporal nature and plenipotent scope of *what* the Great Old Ones and Cthulhu are is limited by something as simple as binding runes? Ancient signs? Please. What does it mean to imprison a thing using sigilized *meaning,* which is all a rune is? A drawing of a line in the sands of Time, an illusory demarcation in a thing that is already an illusion, as the mystics tell us and affirm. To speak of binding a thing is to speak of contracts, and contracts, by their very nature, are *agreements* between parties.

Knowing this, the R'lyehian understands the patience of Cthulhu. Cthulhu waits. Cthulhu dreams. Cthulhu could, in fact, rise at any time; the so-called *bindings* that we are told keeps it in this state are as nothing. Contracts are made to be broken, re-negotiated, tossed aside, at least as much as they are to be held; the contract is a mere arrangement between parties, parties which we can barely conceive of, for reasons that cannot be fathomed by us, not in a thousand strange aeons.

And so the R'lyehian recognizes Cthulhu's patience and seeks to mirror it in their own life and practice. He recognizes his own place, miniscule and as near to meaningless as it is, in the slow, grinding movement of the aforementioned cosmic gear-works. In service to the Lord of Dreams, if the

R'lyehian, through a supreme effort of will and sorcery and directed dreaming, manages to shift a glowing cog a millimeter further along the track that leads to the return of the Great Old Ones, and no further, then *that*? Even *that* is enough for him.

Not for him are the fevered posturings and unthinking propitiations of the lesser minded, for whom the raising of R'lyeh must happen *now*, right this minute, just as soon as this working is complete, this sacrifice made, these barbarous syllables chanted badly into the night. For these lesser ones, Cthulhu is something to be summoned, something outside of themselves which (they feel, erroneously) can be made manifest in their tiny circles of intent. The Platonic ideal of Madness somehow little more than a bogeyman to be whistled for and directed at the enemies of the small-minded. Minds such as these, stultified and walled-in as they are (however colourful and creative the graffiti on those walls), could never contain the enormity of Cthulhu. These minds are *not R'lyehian*, they are merely human and of the most standard type. For all their protestations to the contrary, they have no understanding of what R'lyeh is, believing it to be a *location*, whereas it is no such thing...

R'lyeh is a state of being. And Cthulhu the supreme expression of that state. The R'lyehian seeks to raise R'lyeh, always, unceasingly, but at the same time she recognizes that Cthulhu will awaken when it is ready and not a moment before.

And in the meantime, we wait. We wait, and teach waiting, and pass that quality of infinitesimal patience on down the centuries and the seconds.

Sorcerous Consciousness

Sorcery has been described as the systematic cultivation of enhanced consciousness and its effective deployment in the world of deeds and ideas. For this examination of the essence of what it is to experience sorcerous consciousness as a R'lyehian, we briefly return now to Lovecraft's descriptive terms for Cthulhu: the wings and feelers and chimerical aspects of its mountainous form.

We have already discussed Cthulhu's totemic kinship with the human life wave. I would argue that this very wave is in fact the genetic expression of sorcery. What are we, as a species, if we are not the part of Nature that continually alters its own consciousness, draws forth from the Platonic realm of perfect Forms flawed and mutated approximations? We are the dreaming ape, the magic users, the tools of our tools. Despoilers, yes, but also augmenters, inventors. Nature (and what an arbitrary designation, what a patently absurd concept *that* is!) could not do for herself what we are doing for her. Here we sit at the crinkly, fractal, bleeding edge of complexity on this planet and for all our guilt and useless hand-wringing over the position, we are here for a reason.

To wit: we are sorcerers, each and every one, though the vast majorities are unaware and unappreciative of this status. Of those that are aware, the best of them have Cthulhu as exemplar and guide.

In Cthulhu's pulpy, tentacled head, we are presented with a vision, a model, of the sorcerous mind. Even in an aeons-long dream of death, Cthulhu is aware, hyper-vigilant, and by no means confined to solitary cognitions: it *reaches out constantly*, contacting sleeping dreamers, speaking to its servants via trance, communing with other Great Old Ones across Time and Space. Influencing, always influencing. Here is a model of multi-tasking, of 360° apprehension, of processing diverse strands of information even while in a state of dormancy. Cthulhu's tentacles grasp, taste, touch. They grasp, and they do not let go until the usefulness of the thing grasped has been fully determined.

Cthulhu's form follows the outlines already mentioned, yet this form is by no means a fixed one. Witness the moment in Lovecraft's story when the skipper of the *Alert*, in a frenzy of terror, plunges his craft into Cthulhu's noxious bulk: Cthulhu rendered itself immaterial, took on a gaseous form, and suffered no injury. Fixed, but not fixed, Cthulhu may *prefer* a certain manifestation, but it is not held to that manifestation, particularly if it comes at cost to itself. Malleable, flexible, the rock and the river, there and not-there, as the situation calls. So, too, a certain flexibility of persona is a must for the active sorcerer.

Perhaps there is such a thing as a *core personality*, but who can say for sure? It is this locking down of who and what we are into a construct (cobbled together from personal history as experienced by us and by those close to us; that which we've learned or accepted as true or false; the expectations of our respective societies and cultures and peer groupings) that limit our freedom and ability to move in the world. In the *worlds* available to us.

By all means, assume a core personality, a preferred manifestation, but ensure that it remains soft. Squamous. Malleable. Be ready to shift, at any moment, in any direction, including the directions that cannot be pointed to. *Especially* those directions. The R'lyehian is non-Euclidean in her adaptability: of persona, of action. There in one moment, as a creative, compassionate, or ambivalent member of human society, and gone the next, donning an exo-personality that allows for slipping off between dimensions, performing incomprehensible feats.

Collect names at will. Dedicate a district of the infinite R'lyeh to housing your cloaks and armours, your sorcerous masks. Multiple personality disorder not as disease[1] (or even *disorder*, for that matter) but as lifestyle choice, as fashion statement, as a suite of tools and skins for navigating strange angles.

And if one or many of those skins should be equipped with wings, so much the better.

Imagine yourself down there, R'lyehian. Inhabit, for the briefest of moments, the slumbering form of your Lord. It is not blasphemy to do so; there is space for you there. Endless honeycombed chambers of pure cthonic Being prepared for you, for your multitude of selves, and you are a mite. Less than a mite, you are microbial, but for an impossible moment, imagine yourself more than microbial, more than human, more than temporary. Imagine yourself eternal. Imagine yourself Cthulhu. Feel the gravity of this planet cradle your vast bulk. The weight of the silt of countless millennia bearing down on your still, patient form, a form that is entirely yours to command, composed of strange matter not bound by any laws save your own. Imagine the aeons of Time that you have rested there, at the centre of the twisted hyperspatial labyrinth that is R'lyeh, the First City, the Dreaming City, and you its Prime Dreamer. Feel the infinite weight of your patience.

Know the secret activity of every mind in the Universe. Taste their dreams as they alight upon your dormant consciousness like dread moths burning to ash. Speak with the others like you, the Great Old Ones in their chambers and prisons and tucked-away folds of Time and Space, speak with them in sentences that see species and civilizations rise and fall into dust. Speak of that moment when the stars are once again right.

And when they are right (and they will be, coming round again in the cycle of Eternity, turning so that you and the others like you will live again) rise, O Madness. Rise, Great Cthulhu, astride the peaks of your city as it breaks the surface of the sea. Rise and open your unspeakably ancient eyes to the sight of a planet consumed in a holocaust of ecstasy and freedom...

R'lyehian. You have wings. You have wings, and the sky and stars of a Universe that has not seen your kind awake in vigintillions of years stretches wide before you.

What are you going to *do*?

Well, exactly.

This, then, is the essence of sorcerous consciousness: to patiently gather power, pull everything that exists into the dark bowers of a mind made

---

1   see the chapter *Beating Nietzsche's Horse*

more-than-spacious by the Black Gnosis, and then to rise, and once risen...
to fly. Every R'lyehian aspires to this state-of-Being, this mirroring (yes, on
our own microbial scale, but a mirroring nonetheless) of the Ascent of our
Lord. The R'lyehian seeks to know Cthulhu, to embody the Black Gnosis,
and this knowing, this becoming, renders the R'lyehian a *cthulhusattva*.

The Cthulhusattva Vow

A Universe of beings imprisoned by Reason
I vow to liberate them all

Delusions of Order and Sanity are inexhaustible
I vow to break them all

Gates to R'lyeh are without number
I vow to enter them all

Cthulhu waits there, dreaming
I vow to raise R'lyeh

A Tour of R'lyeh

In my persona as anti-poet and spoken-word artist skawt chonzz, I put out a slim, limited-run chapbook early in 2011, *R'lyeh Sutra,* which had as its sometime theme the Black Gnosis itself. From the introduction...

> The drowned hyper-opolis of R'lyeh, vast and terrible, beyond rational understanding, boiling with fractal connectivity and vibrating on every level of so-called Reality (R'lyeh-ity, if we're to be painfully honest, and we are), its non-Euclidean architecture an assault on lower-order mammalian perception, its migraine towers and impossible arches and obsidian middens awash in the febrile submarine light that characterizes the depths of the Unconscious.

> R'lyeh! The first city, the dreaming city, the mad city of unspoken terrors and fevered ecstasies. R'lyeh! The infinite suburbs of existential mirror-muck, sprawling slums constructed of discarded, croaking anti-languages, laced over with living circuitry telepathically transmitting a constant insect-chitter stream of flash-cut reverse-universe pornography. R'lyeh! Suppurating districts of

unspeakable shopping malls that give ferocious new meaning to consumption and thumping hyper-dimensional everlasting-night clubs, every bouncer a shoggoth, every dancer a coruscating chaos of perversion and alien sensuality. R'lyeh! Mausoleum and corpse-throne capital city of Great Cthulhu, Lord of Dreams, High Priest of All That Is Not, of the Forgotten Ones and Those Who Whisper Behind the Light. Cthulhu, who is dead but dreaming.

R'lyeh.

My home.

Upon my death, drop my cold flesh at these coordinates - 47° 9' S 126° 43' W - and let me sink through green leagues to that place where thought is obliterated, where form is plastic, where dreams are solid and unyielding as stone. There will I wait, in that lair of the untranslatable, for the return of the Great Old Ones and the remaking of the world in fire and in ice. I will rise with R'lyeh when the stars come right.

The shamans who work their primal magics in the Bon-po tradition of Tibetan Buddhism undergo what they call the chöd ritual, in which the body is brutally dismembered by wrathful demons. In this way they learn to not identify with the physical, to transcend the limitations of the material. From this, and from our own wracked imagination-factories, we can infer that there is enlightenment in horror, and in the extremes of fear may be found a moment of pure, one-pointed awareness. That awe-full clarity.

This is the Black Gnosis: when all is madness, there is no madness.

In the summer of 2011, just after our first child was born, my wife decided that she wanted to get a tattoo that celebrated her hometown of Vancouver, that energetic jewel-cluster of green-blue glass, steel, and cedar-wood in the boreal crown of the Pacific Rim. She hit upon the idea of having the coordinates, the latitude and longitude that pinned Vancouver to the globe, inked in black on the top of her left foot. It was a charming conception: a line of numbers and letters, degrees and minutes filling the soft flesh between her fourth and fifth metatarsal ligaments.

"You know, in case I'm ever abducted by aliens and taken off-planet," she said. "This way they'll know where to return me."

At the shop, under the needle, as I bounced our three-month old son on my knee, my wife turned to me and asked whether I would get something similar. (We do tend to collect ink, as a couple, and it's become something of an arms race in recent years. Yes, it's probably a generational thing.[1]) Which coordinates were *home* for me?

"Oh, it's wherever my family is at. It's with you and the boy here."

"Yes, but *where?* I'm looking for a location here!"

"You know I've never felt at home anywhere. It's not a feeling I recognize anywhere..."

This is very true. I've lived most of my life in one of the more beautiful spots on this planet, and have traveled enough to know quite a few more, but even so, no one place has ever engendered in me that feeling of *home.* Which is not to say that I don't feel a certain home*sickness* at times. That, at least, is a feeling I'm familiar with, something akin to Lovecraft's *intense nostalgia,* but not for a place. This feeling is for a state of being. And it is only lessened when I enter into R'lyehian consciousness, when I descend into the Black Gnosis that lies at the core of my awareness.

47° 9' S 126° 43' W

These coordinates now describe a gentle arc across my chest, beneath the collarbone. At the very least, I can open my shirt and point to this ink whenever the question "where is your god now?" is asked of me by smug atheists. My wife likes to joke that it should help with my cred should I ever find myself in prison...

"You'll probably be raped less," she says.

"Maybe initially," I reply. "Until someone actually looks that location up. Then I'll be raped *more.*"

It's a risk I'm willing to take.

Does the dreaming necropolis of R'lyeh, the vast mausoleum city of Cthulhu *actually exist* at those coordinates in the cold seeps of the Pacific? My future cell block *paramours* would likely claim "no" and on the surface,

---

1   And yes, I'm winning.

I would certainly agree with them. The ocean floor there is the ocean floor: silt, organic till, stone. There is nothing down there. Nothing at all.

And it is within that Nothing that R'lyeh lives.

R'lyeh is a super-contextual city. The ignorant ask where it is, but the wise know the better question to be *where is it not?* Lovecraft, in an attempt to sound mystical, wrote of the Great Old Ones as existing "not in the spaces we know, but between them": the negative spaces, the mirror-Universe, the reverse of the Tree. Call it what you like, their lives are lived in the hollow-ness of That Which Is, in the void that defines That Which Is Not. Should we expect their cities to not share in that self-same manner of existence?

R'lyeh is *everywhere*[1]. It is *the* Eternal City, of which all other cities are but shadows cast into Time. Every habitation of conscious beings is a reflec-tion of some small part of R'lyeh, the tower blocks and avenues and shops merely the reduced and refracted Euclidean manifestation of some larger, non-Euclidean monolith or concourse or waste-midden of R'lyeh. The Black Gnosis which is its power and lifeblood oozes through to our urban environ-ments in the lineaments of viral advertising. It lays slick and sentient in the shadows cast down alleyways, pulses between the strobing flicker of fluo-rescent tubes in abandoned cubicle farms, hitches rides on the underside of the random verbal foamings of the transient population. Late night walks through your city with no pre-determined destination are always transfor-mative, enlightening, profoundly unsettling. The conscientious R'lyehian makes these midnight meanderings a habit.

All well and good, surely, but what *is* R'lyeh? It is everywhere, yes, but putting pads to pavement in the pre-dawn precincts of Peoria or Paris or Pyongyang will not necessarily take one there, for R'lyeh is present as a kind of potential. R'lyeh and its inhabitant[2] are, as (one version of) the Necronomicon states, "even as one with your guarded threshold". This could (and in a few carefully kept cases, does) reference actual gates, physical entryways into horrific zones of pure gnosis. But often as not, the portal to the Dreaming City is psychic in nature.

R'lyeh rises in every heart, but before this can happen, the R'lyehian must make of their mind a suburb of that great city. The ground must be prepared. To do so, one must identify the "guarded threshold" within the labyrinthine coils of one's own mind. The R'lyehian asks of herself "where

---

1   Perhaps this would account for the R'lyehian never experiencing a sense of "home" in the world: if all cities are R'lyeh at some hidden level, then the R'lyehian is always home and would not necessarily long for another place, or place more value on one city over another.

2   Indeed, all of the Great Old Ones.

can I not go within myself? Which doors are closed, locked, kept under watch by sentries of shifting light and shadow?" She asks these things in all seriousness and when the answers come (as they must do, as they are in fact *eager* to do, for a door unopened is unfulfilled in its purpose), when those gates are identified and swing wide at the lightest touch, she steps across her guarded threshold and through, through to R'lyeh.

If it can be cognized at all, R'lyeh may be thought of as an anti-memory palace or mandala, with Cthulhu and the Black Gnosis which is its gift at the core of its shifting heart. Access to it occurs through a kind of *gestalt* apprehension of every awful, terrifying, or unsettling recollection: not necessarily your own memories (though these can and should be used, if applicable) but also genetic memory, species memory. Memories not your own and from all points on the space-time super-sphere: that moment your band of proto-primates was absorbed into a steaming plasmic mass that oozed from beneath a granite slab, the shock of surprised recognition when some distant ancestor beheld their own face in a mirror and saw someone else, the first time the Sun went nova. Faceplates cracking in deep vacuum. Disturbing graffitos glowing in the nave of an abandoned church.

The possible locations of all these memories (the above being only a few random selections, pulled, appropriately, from the air, from Nothing) and an infinitude of others are all present within the super-structural negative-matrices that make up R'lyeh. They dance and slide as viscous oils across vast non-Euclidean planes of unthinkable thoughts. They float silently as mirrored spheres of quicksilver in depths of eternal blackness and pressure. These are the winged and fanged memories that eat themselves, primal ouroboroi all, churning out the pure ichor of Cthulhu's dread dreaming from their unhallowed orifices. The flagstones and columns and alleys of R'lyeh are coated in a fine, fine silt composed of the remains of all possible recollections, atomized, reduced to the barest quanta of experience.

If you have ever been startled out of a deep sleep, gasping for air, unsure, for a few panicked seconds, of who or even what you were, your head filled with hypnagogic visions of things never experienced by you and yet utterly real seeming, like a memory, then know that you have ingested a particle of R'lyehian atmosphere in your sleep. It is these particles, this sleep-silt, which must be conscientiously and carefully gathered and spread upon the surface of the R'lyehian awareness, as mortar for the laying down of the tiles that will cover your own personal prefecture of the mighty city itself.

R'lyeh rises in every heart, true, but it (or at least that infinitesimally small portion of it which allows us access to the greater bulk) is *built* in the mind. R'lyehian, make of your mind a suburb. Know, and dare to pry open the gates of your guarded thresholds, and step through into wonder and glory. Never know homesickness again.

Take the tour, and become one with R'lyeh.

The Black Gnosis

When all is madness
There is no madness

The Black Gnosis is the supreme jewel of attainment for those who would pursue a life of R'lyehian spirituality, a R'lyehian consciousness. It is a knowledge, deeply felt and internalized, not of That Which Is, but of That Which Is Not; a profoundly instinctual apprehension of the liminal spaces, in-between-ness, and porosity of the world, of the Unknown. For the R'lyehian, the Black Gnosis begins with fear of the Unknown (the greatest of fears), as is only natural, but she does not linger there, indulging in animal panic; she moves beyond and through fear to a paradoxical "knowing" of the Unknown.

The Black Gnosis is Black, not in a dull dualistic or Satanic sense (world-views that are intrinsically tied to an anthropocentric philosophy), but Black in the sense that it is not born of rationality, of the logical parsing out of one thing from another, of any of the divisive concerns that could be considered human. The Black Gnosis arises from and constantly partakes of the undifferentiated and chaotic ground of being. It is a gnosis of the Gulf, of the Empty.

The Black Gnosis is the unthinkable thought on the bleeding edge of trying to think itself. It is the very essence of Cthulhu's dream, and if the

R'lyehian is lucky it will touch her mind and make changes therein. The Black Gnosis is a gnosis of the dark between the stars, of the void-spaces, of the gap and the crevice, the tube and the abyss. It is porous, shot through with vacuity, a true mirror of the universe itself, all yawning gulfs and vast howling nothing.

As such, it fills the mind by *not filling it at all,* instead mapping its own living emptiness onto the infinite surface area of all that you are not aware of. Are you ignorant? Oh yes. Will all your striving to change that reduce your ignorance by one jot? No. The larger you build the bonfire, the more darkness it reveals. The R'lyehian knows this, but does not use it as an excuse to shrink from the acquisition of knowledge: straining in every direction (including the ones that cannot be pointed to), she seeks to increase the surface area of her ignorance. The R'lyehian is, perforce, an omnivorous auto-didactic polymath engaged in a constant "correlating of the contents", open to all information, all data, all ideas, and she will swim any sea. She desires only to bathe in the deadly light...

> *... but some day the piecing together of dissociated knowledge will open up such terrifying vistas of reality, and of our frightful position therein, that we shall either go mad from the revelation or flee from the deadly light into the peace and safety of a new dark age.*
>
> — H. P. Lovecraft, *The Call of Cthulhu*

The light reveals, and it drives one to madness... but it *still reveals!* Apocalypse is apocalypse, whatever its form, and the things revealed, however frightful, are at the least true things. The R'lyehian does not flee that light, he enters. He embraces. And if in that embracing he is seen as mad by those who would prefer sane and peaceful darkness, then so be it. Better to lose a mind than waste it in the pursuit of falseness. Or rather, better to *loose* it into the freedom and revelry of unmitigated and un-blinkered perception, into knowledge.

The Black Gnosis *is* madness, yes, and that madness is infinite and all-engulfing and will consume a mind in order to free it, but the R'lyehian recognizes that there is nothing there to be consumed in the first place. The R'lyehian recognizes that Thought and Mind are merely epiphenomenal vapours arising from the surface of the Black Gnosis itself. The Black Gnosis is the ground of all, and when *all* is madness, there is no madness: there is only the true nature of reality, what some might term *the horror of our situation*, Lovecraft's "frightful position". The R'lyehian, though, in attaining the Black Gnosis, has moved beyond horror, beyond the spastic monkey agitation that seizes the unprepared and the unregenerate when faced with the felt revelations regarding our place in the Void. Felt, because it is one thing to spin words like spider-silk around the Black Gnosis (as I am forced to do here, recognizing at all times the utter futility of my actions – the Zen aphorism "this book is a wasted effort" certainly applies here), and quite another to feel it.

The R'lyehian has moved beyond animal horror and can appraise himself calmly in the reversed-light of the Black Gnosis; recognize and even be amused by the scrap of Is-ness that he appears to be. *I am It, and It is I. Light is dark and dark is light.*[1] Is there peace to be had there, in the "deadly light"? After a fashion, yes. What is killed, when that light is entered? Only illusion. Only the perception of that which perceives. The eyes open as the I opens, and the R'lyehian meets the gaze of the awakened Cthulhu, as in a mirror, and is consumed. All rationality burns away. And what dreams follow, who can tell? Only other R'lyehians, those who have entered the Black Gnosis and returned to take the Cthulhusattva Vow.

How may these be recognized? It is, admittedly, a difficult thing to pick a R'lyehian out of the teeming horde: not only that of general humanity, but of the Lovecraftian hangers-on and standard-issue weirdos. The Black Gnosis is, naturally, stealthy. A pure mimic. There's camouflage, and then there's *camouflage*, and the Black Gnosis is most definitely of the latter variety. Pretenders will wear their "madness" on their sleeves; they will cloak themselves in seeming weirdness for all the world to gawk at. Probably this satisfies them on some strictly human level: the posturing, the public play-acting, the unspeakable rites, the t-shirts and jewelry, books and conventions and the endless, tiresome stream of Lovecraftian products. The R'lyehian has no time for this. The R'lyehian leaves them to it.

One thing is certain: you will not recognize a R'lyehian by their seeming madness. R'lyeh lives and rises, not in the readily apparent things of a person, in their traits and foibles and outward, armoured display of character, but in the spaces between those things. Many R'lyehians present to the world a completely benign, utterly normal countenance and lifestyle. They feel no need to disengage from the world, to dress up, to posture, all in order to show their uniqueness, to flaunt a cherished Outsider status. To do so is to ritualize existence, and that way lies cult and ignorance. Ritual is fine if the

---

1   *The Haunter of the Dark*, H.P. Lovecraft

practitioner *does not know what she is doing.* The R'lyehian, however, always strives to know, to dive, to get to the essence of the thing, and so quickly leaves all poses behind. To pose is to become stiff, unyielding, and the R'lyehian is ever fluid, syncretic, a shapeshifter of the first water.

There is something to be said here, too, for the thrill of cognitive dissonance that the true R'lyehian consciousness brings as it condenses on the surfaces of identity. For instance, I am, on any number of apparent surfaces, each facet catching and reflecting the light of awareness, many things: a husband and father, son and brother, a healer, a writer, a poet... and it is these facets, these Things That Are Me, that act as the borders of the Things That Are Not Me. Borders which are, at times, alarmingly porous. I (or at least the cross-section of Space/Time that organizes as I) am a thousand white-hot compartments, each filled with nameless things, unthinkable thoughts, contradictory cognitions. And of these un-things, I am always aware; they are never far from the surface. They press against the membranes, constantly testing the edges, not for weakness, but for *agreement*. This surface tension, then, is utterly pleasurable, and informs my existence without necessarily deforming it. My life is lived, not in contrast to That Which Is Not, but in con*text*.

In short, I *am* weird, and profoundly so, but you would never know it to meet me in person. At least, not in the early days of our association. Even my physical and aesthetic presentation would throw you off: I have a fondness for well-tailored summer weight suits and pocket squares, and I keep my hair short and professionally styled. This (at least for me, for now) is the R'lyehian way, a path of mimicry and camouflage. It is not a way of the things on the surface; it is a way of the deeps, of the Void. The Black Gnosis fills the interstitial spaces, which are infinite. And we are *all interstitial space*. What little of us that *can* be seen is but a gloss, a rough collection of sticks and forest litter concealing the pit; it is of little importance to the interior life.

I have mentioned how the Black Gnosis tends to condense on the surface of the R'lyehian's character: when it does, it often manifests as three traits or marks, three modes of expression or ways of moving through and interacting with the world which are immediately felt and apprehended as true on many levels, but particularly on the somatic, the level of the meat. These modes are Horror (the *Chill*), Humour (the *Grin*), and Lust (the *Burning Gaze*)[1].

---

1   Incidentally, as a writer, I find that when these modes are employed in a piece of fiction, the measure of success is felt on the somatic level as well. When I write something frightening, I know it, because I feel fear. If I laugh, then I know I've written something funny. And sexual arousal during or after the penning of some smut is a sure sign of the effectiveness of the work. These are sensations common to all.

It has been said that terror is the feared thing unseen but anticipated, and that Horror is the feared thing finally seen and understood to be far worse than the anticipation: there are obvious parallels here between Faith and Knowledge, in the biblical sense. In any case, there is a moment, in the early stages of attaining the Black Gnosis, when the awful truth of this definition (and the feeling it defines) strikes with all the lashing, howling ferocity of a hurricane. The *horror of our situation,* of our place in the cosmos, hits home, and when it does all pretence to rationality, to prominence, to potency (as an individual, as a species), evaporates, leaving only the *Chill,* the somatic sensation associated with Horror. It evaporates and more importantly, it *never returns,* except as a useful suite of tools, a social framework or game-theory, a set of agreements for interacting with others. The R'lyehian, in attaining the Black Gnosis and becoming a vehicle for it, is able to embody and express this Horror in such a way as to *make others feel it.*

This does not mean striking a pose, going for the cheap scare that is easily seen through and laughed off. Nor does it mean retreating into a sulking, defeated nihilism. No, there is a certain glee associated with this Horror; the dark joy of meeting the divine and knowing it as completely Other. To dream with Cthulhu is to empty oneself of all pre-conceived human dreams, to sink into depths of greater Dream, of greater Horror: the R'lyehian continually exposes herself to that storm of revelation, she lives and breathes within it. So, when the opportunity presents itself, she exhales Horror into a conversation or an interaction. This may take the form of a frosty observation on the nature of Mind, or a dropped fact regarding some scientific or cosmological truth, or an anecdote that reveals, momentarily, the churning, gnosis-rich voids within her own person. This exhalation is not constant, or even consistent, which only adds to the chilling power of the thing when it happens.

This is also accomplished through actions that defy social and intellectual strictures, the doing of things that make no sense. I am reminded here of the Borges tale *The Lottery of Babylon,* in which the random outcomes of various impersonal drawings in the titular lottery (a jewel thrown in a river, a bird released from a certain roof at a certain hour, or a grain of sand added or removed from a beach) can have terrifying consequences.

The R'lyehian is a contagion vector, if you will, for the Black Gnosis; dropping into conversations, when the opportunity presents itself, bizarre and unsettling facts (scientific, occult, or otherwise) regarding the cosmos and our place in it. At all times, or at unexpected times (which can be more effective), the R'lyehian exhales the *Chill* of the Black Gnosis into relationships and interactions.

This exhalation is not without its amusement, though: for the R'lyehian, Humour is the twin of Horror. Having exposed himself to Horror, and passed through it, the R'lyehian is, as commonly expressed, "in on the joke". Dagon's Teeth! What other option does he *have*, knowing what he knows and feeling what he feels? Dagon's Teeth, indeed: the pure expression of R'lyehian Humour, the *Grin* that arises from the Black Gnosis. Following swiftly on the *Chill* of Horror comes the *Grin*, which can range anywhere from a smile of compassionate, situational solidarity with other humans (whether they are in on the joke or not) to a rictus of insane mirth in the psychic presence of the Great Old Ones. This laughter in the full glare of the deadly light is perhaps the only truly "sane" response to the Black Gnosis; it is non-dual, it has no opposing emotion or response, it is utterly pure and freeing.

Although it can be mistaken for an expression of nihilism, the *Grin* is not a cynical one. Nihilism is in so many ways a defensive response to existence, a donning of bitter existential armour against the meaninglessness of the cosmos. Within that armour, the creature of Nihil rots and desiccates and in so doing, somehow imagines itself safe and wise. The R'lyehian laughs and drops all protection, opening herself to the storm of being, to all that waits Outside of herself. This is a radical opening as well, not some milquetoast expression along the lines of "yeah, I'm open to it. I have an open mind" that one hears so often from self-described liberal types when they only wish to let you know that their boundaries lie just that little bit further out than others. The *Grin* laughs at boundaries, rockets past them in half a heartbeat. The *Grin* serves as a vehicle of desire, the teeth gnashing to feed upon new knowledge, new experience, and meaning be damned. The *Grin* is power, delight, and humble glee in the face of the unspeakable. Know the R'lyehian by her smile.

Know her, also, by her Lust, by her *Burning Gaze*. The R'lyehian takes a profound interest in the machinations of desire: her own and those of others. The *Burning Gaze* recalls the ecstatic connection of the Sufi; a true R'lyehian can get off on the sight of a glass of water. In the act of apprehending a thing, whatever that thing may be (place, object, person, concept) the R'lyehian enters into a strange (and in many ways blasphemous, if "blasphemy" is that which offends the restrictive, rational powers at work in the world) coupling, not so much with the thing itself, its solidity or its obvious traits, but with that which the thing is not. There is a hole in everything, and the R'lyehian seeks to enter that vacancy, to fill it and become it at the same time.

There is no knowing a thing without a becoming of that thing: this is the consuming truth that drives the expression of Lust that lies behind the *Burning Gaze*. We want, always, and what we want is that which we are not. Achieving this, the R'lyehian necessarily causes the lusted after thing to cease to be as itself, for it is now him. This is a mad hunger: for sex, for sensation, for information, and for new ways of experiencing and combining these things. In this way, the R'lyehian anticipates the rising of R'lyeh and the awakening of Cthulhu, that moment when all the earth will "flame with a holocaust of ecstasy and freedom". The word, *holocaust*, is Greek in origin, and has the base meaning of "sacrifice by fire": in this case (in all cases, perhaps?) the fire of Lust.

And what is sacrificed in those flames? Again, as when the R'lyehian enters the deadly light, merely illusion: the fabrications of self, the fragile scaffolding of ego and history. The seemingly solid mass of That Which Is gives way to a profound ungrounding, and is seen to be riddled through with That Which Is Not.

So, when presented with an opportunity to direct the *Burning Gaze* upon a situation, the answer to the question "well, what do I have to lose?" is obvious to the R'lyehian: nothing. Nothing at all.

That being said, it should be noted that the Black Gnosis (this living madness that moves through and behind the R'lyehian existence, informing and shaping it) is not a reductive madness. The R'lyehian does not shrink back into herself as a result of contact with the Black Gnosis. The Black Gnosis does not remove elements from her life but adds to it, constantly. It is a heaping of things, a constant expansion of knowledge and sensation, of data, a never-ending piling of wood and bones and smoking sacrificial meat upon the bonfire of experience. The Black Gnosis does not retreat; it is an upwardly mobile madness. When the stars are right, R'lyeh (the capital of all That Is Not) rises: towards greater complexity, greater connection, greater involvement with all That Is.

The void penetrates and permeates the solid, and there's always plenty of solid to go around.

When all is madness (which is to say when all is *seen* to be madness, when our frightful position is fully appreciated, accepted, and assimilated), there is no madness...

Beating Nietzsche's Horse:
Notes on the Black Gnosis
and Mental Illness

Madness need not be all breakdown. It may also be break-through. It is potential liberation and renewal as well as enslavement and existential death.

— R D Laing

It's important to make a distinction between the essence of what the Black Gnosis is and the effects, behavioural changes and symptoms arising from common mental illness. Though the two states share certain similarities, and the behaviours of R'lyehians and the mentally ill can seem, on the surface, to be drawn from the same pool, the two states of being could not be more different. This difference arises in approach, and in the choices made once one has passed into the Black Gnosis and, necessarily, gone beyond good and evil, as per Nietzsche.

We've all met them, of course, those hapless souls haunted by Nietzsche's ghost. The Overmen (and sometimes women, though tellingly not often) of the coffee shop and the kitchen party. Burdened by their less-than-comprehensive understanding of his philosophy, and in their insistence on moving beyond what they *perceive* to be good and evil, they trap themselves in a bitter and ineffectual mental space. They imagine themselves free, and noble, but that imagining is as far as it goes. Often, these faux-Nietzschian's are in it for far less noble reasons, utilizing the man's work as a justification for any number of poor behaviours, sad transgressions of a perceived status quo, executions of awkward dance moves around hated morals that they cannot move beyond except through soft-headed pseudo-rebellions.

But who among these are truly game to go where Nietzsche went, in the end? Who will find themselves in the middle of the street, their arms wrapped around the foaming neck of a beaten horse, their minds bleeding away into the ether with the sorrow and the horror of it all? For that was the philosopher's end, his breaking point, right there. A point followed by a malingering period of penning mad letters to friends and family, and eventually death in a sanitarium.

Sad, deluded Overfolk! Here then is the punch line to your favourite quote: at the critical moment, Nietzsche blinked.

He blinked, and in so doing, missed the one action of the Abyss that the R'lyehian, the cultivator of the Black Gnosis, waits for with gleeful anticipation: that sublime moment when the Abyss gazes back... *and winks.*[1]

We are, as Lewis Carrol's Cheshire cat affirms, "all mad here"[2]. The very fact that you are *here* speaks to this essential truth. To choose to incarnate in the first place is to choose to enter into suffering and death, joy and weirdness. Life is an acquired taste, to be sure, and will defend its own viewpoint. Life will rally any number of apparently rational arguments against the supreme irrationality of itself. To the death, usually.

So, we are here, alive and mad and standing before a miserable horse in the street. What's to be done about it?

The difference between a mentally ill person and their insanity, and a R'lyehian and her madness, her cultivation of the Black Gnosis, then, is this: the insane person is not free to act. They are locked down into their disease, whether that disease has a biological, pharmacological, or

---

1 How is this "winking" of the Abyss differentiated from the winking mentioned in the Introduction to this book? Quite simply, the latter is a kind of whistling-past-the-graveyard, a wink that speaks volumes regarding our species predilection for not-noticing our "frightful position". Are we embedded in a cosmos of unfeeling, chaotic principles of being and manifestation? Why yes, but here's an odd Lovecraftian monster to embody such principles and take your mind off it, says that wink, favoured by blind atheists and the shallowly religious alike. The former wink, the Primal Wink of which I speak here, the Wink of the Abyss after a long, hard, appraising stare, is of a different order entirely. The latter is a nervous giggle at a poorly understood pun, the former is a mad guffaw of acceptance and enlightenment as one bathes in the deadly light of the ultimate Joke.

2 "But I don't want to go among mad people," Alice remarked.
"Oh, you can't help that," said the Cat: "we're all mad here. I'm mad. You're mad."
"How do you know I'm mad?" said Alice.
"You must be," said the Cat, "or you wouldn't have come here."
-- Lewis Carroll, *Alice in Wonderland*

psychological origin. They cannot move beyond the confines of their sickness[1] and are quick to manacle themselves to reductive reasonings that explain their behaviours.

The R'lyehian, though mad (and thoroughly so!) is free to act, from and into his madness, and actively uses the Black Gnosis to do his work in the world. As has been mentioned elsewhere, the madness of the R'lyehian is *stealthy* and does not call attention to itself; cultivating and activating the Black Gnosis should not be a trigger for the so-called sane members of society to call for the white van in alarm. "Sane" members of society stay that way through a process of not-noticing; the R'lyehian insures that the sane are in no way perturbed or agitated, and goes about his business[2].

And the difference between a R'lyehian and the average Nietzschean Over-schlub? The simplest of distinctions: Humour. The R'lyehian has passed beyond good and evil, perhaps in ways that the Nietzschean will never be able to do. She *is* Friedrich's dancing star, giving birth to herself from chaos. She has not flinched from the winking of the Abyss and has made love to her monsters. The Black Gnosis has her, and its gift is the Grin.

---

1 Too often "disease" and "sickness" are the prime descriptors used by both the medical community (who are philosophically and professionally aligned to this view) and society-at-large for any and all symptoms of madness. I am reminded of the recent memoir by New York Post columnist Susannah Cahalan, *Brain On Fire: My Month of Madness*, in which she details the fight to retrieve her mind and life from the ravages of a little-known auto-immune disorder.

Cahalan (and perhaps not surprisingly, her doctors) claim that the disease is the cause of "demonic possessions" throughout history. I posit here that a twenty-something tabloid journalist and yes, her attendant medical professionals (with all due respect to their learning and skills) are hardly in a position to *know* from demonic possession one way or the other, are they? Here, the destructive path of a disease through the meat of a person, a path that results in behavioural change, is equated with madness: a too-easy label to apply.

Madness is madness, the Black Gnosis is the Black Gnosis, and disease is disease. Let us call each what it is, for what it is, and avoid confusion.

2 Perturbing and agitating normal people is the easiest thing in the world, after all. It takes no skill or special effort and is a task regularly performed by teenagers and those who enjoy negative attention. The R'lyehian's ego is a loosely consolidated mass of particles, porous and light: what need does she have of the clucking attention of the mundane?

Beyond the Strange Angles

R'lyehian spirituality is an experience that is largely divorced from the trappings of standard magical and religious systems. R'lyehian thought and spirituality is, for the most part, an internally experienced phenomenon. The fact remains, however, that occasions characterized by what could be termed a *higher intensity* of that experience do happen. At these moments, what does R'lyehian practice look like? How does it manifest for the practitioner, externally? What, if anything, do observers on such occasions experience? In an effort to answer these questions, I offer the following account as a small and by no means exhaustive example of how such a moment may play out. The two remaining chapters in this section deal with the R'lyehian current of artistic practice.

Chilling in the Ghetto with the Deep Down Homies

An evening in August. Dusk has fallen, the sky is in that odd threshold state where it can't seem to decide what to be, the shallow flatness of daylight blue giving way to purple depths, the first stars beginning to blink in the wells of night. I'm in a cab that's circling a park that lies between the city and the shore. On the seat next to me is a backpack stuffed with an assortment of gear, practical and esoteric: smudge pots, lighters, small halogen spotlights, two Tibetan singing bowls, a pair of Baoding balls, cigars, water, a prayer mat and monk's stool, a bottle of whiskey, and an asymmetrical leather fetish mask in the shape of an octopus, the tentacles stiff with disuse. It's been a while since I've had occasion to wear the mask, and I'm nervous, jittery.

I'm waiting for something, some sign showing me where to have the driver pull over. Or I *think* I'm waiting for something. In the end, it's much of a muchness, that distinction, and the driver decides for me...

"This is the third time around. Want me to go again?"

I shrug, tell him to stop. As signs go, it's enough. What was I really waiting for, I wonder. Sufficient for each night its own weirdness, and there is weirdness enough to come. He pulls over, and as I pay him I reflect on my last-minute choice to take a cab here. The original plan had been to hoof it across town, through the park, and down to the shore, a light trek that would not have been all that exhausting, but, considering the rigours of the night before me, an unnecessary drain on my strength and resources. I'm glad of the cab, and only mildly surprised to see that I've been dropped not far from where I would have emerged from the park, had I walked.

The cab pulls away. I cross the empty road in the gloom and set my feet to the dry scratch of a trail that passes through the yellow cedar brush and Garry oak scrub that clusters at the cliff edge, the vegetation still warm and fragrant from the long summer day. Heated saps and salt air tang carried on the cooling breath from below; the air smells like candy and rot, a strangely intoxicating mix. I find a branching trail that drops quickly to a rough stairway of planks before finally giving way to a beach of jumbled black rocks and bleached driftwood.

It's getting dark now. The moon won't rise for several hours and when it does it's going to be a slip of a thing, barely waxed at all, but I'm not worried, as I can do the set-up for this in my sleep, really. It's August 20: Lovecraft's birthday. Like the barbaric name of his prime creation, the date means something and nothing; it's a place holder only, a point in Time, useful for marking a moment and little else. Two years before, my wife and I hosted a Lovecraftian movie night for close friends. Last year, I spent several months and not-a-few dollars creating a "Lovecraft's 120th Birthday Celebration and Cthulhu-riffic Cabaret", complete with readings, live theatre, comedy acts, and an exclusive screening of David Prior's excellent short film *AM1200*.

Tonight is different. Tonight is a re-connection, a sacrament. I start walking, picking my way across boulders and leftover glacial till, not thinking or feeling in any sort of way that could be recognized as such. I'm walking *into* sorcerous consciousness, walking in the gathering dark towards a state of being.

I don't know where I'll stop. If I've any criteria in mind at all for the spot, it's that it be relatively flat, with enough room to set up the resonators. After a while of mindless wandering, I hit upon a place: a bare expanse of sandstone, a headland or point of sorts, backed by a crumbling cliff of dry earth and scrubby black Scotch broom, fairly reeking of creosote. I lower the pack to the ground. It's completely dark by now, and as I kick around the spot, moving loose stones and driftwood with my feet, I discern the rough outline of what seems to be a rectangular pit at the western edge of the flat area, and what appear to be the remains of concrete pilings at the corners of the pit. I recall that this part of the shore used to house gun emplacements during WWII. The weapons have long since been removed, leaving these abandoned constructions wearing away into the surrounding environment. I dig around in my pack, remove one of the halogen spots, cast light into the pit: seawater and garbage, a vague bristling shape that could be the remains of some animal. A used condom. Crushed beer cans flashing like the exposed sides of beached fish. Life, death, lust, the whole ridiculous shebang. Perfect.

I turn off the spot, get down on my hands and knees and bark the sound of explosive shells rocketing off into the night, imagining unpleasant bone-and-sinew projectiles loaded with alien toxins exiting the barrel of my throat, hissing out over the water, clearing the Olympic Mountains on the far side of the Straight, dropping into the wide Pacific.

This is the spot. This will do. I start to unpack.

I surround the area with resonators: the simplest of upright wire frames, their bases held down by stones, to which I clip pages of channeled script. The spots are positioned to shine on the paper. No matter where I will turn tonight, I will have concrete examples of my deeply personal dream-conduit before my eyes. This is in case I find the human parts of myself attempting sad rationalizations in the dark, throwing up barricades of shameful reason against the Black Gnosis. I lay out the prayer rug, ensure that the monk's stool is stable on the cooling rock beneath it, and arrange the singing bowls and various liquids and smoking materials around me. I take off my pea-coat, remove my street clothes, change into a pair of loose Thai fisherman's pants and nothing else. A stiff wind is blowing off the water, the heat of the day quickly dissipating. It may be August, but this is the Pacific Rim, and it's going to be a cold night. I'm committed to riding it out, though, to feel every shiver and shake, to know my bones by their blue glow through my skin.

I understand that I may have guests for the evening. Random beach wanderers, the homeless, the drunk and the high, perhaps even a few friends and acquaintances: I have, after all, not made a secret of my activities this night. I've never understood the elitist vetting of potential participants the more traditional practitioners perform before their rites. I praise and welcome the random influx of strange, contradictory energy: if the thing invoked is flustered and unable to respond when presented with elements of pure chance, what good is it? How powerful is it, really? No, let them come. I am opening an etheric corridor to a R'lyehian ghetto tonight, or at least, that's what it says on the Facebook event page, along with a general location. *Somewhere between this point of land and that one.* If interested parties can find me, let them find me. Let them add their tensions, their pulsing neuroses to this transmission. Let them receive as I receive.

Folding my legs beneath the stool, I take a long pull from the whiskey, light a smudge pot, and place a Baoding ball in one of the singing bowls. With one hand holding the bowl from below and the other covering the top with spread fingers, I proceed to slowly rotate the bowl before me in a horizontal plane. The heavy metal sphere begins to roll against the inner surface of the bowl and an awful antiphonal ringing begins, accompanied by a grinding rattle as metal chips away at metal. The sound moves out across the water, is returned to me altered by the reflecting topographies of wave and rock and god-knows-what else. I let it fade, remove the now warm ball, and, picking up a pestle, give the bowl a solid strike to its edge. A clear ring, this time, and a pure, almost exquisite chill travels up my spine. I take another swallow of whiskey.

There is no *beginning* to these things. The R'lyehian existence is one of constant background signal. Moments like these, nights such as this (whether planned or not), are merely an increase in gain on that signal: I am simply turning up the dial. Cthulhu dreams, whether we join it in that dream or not. So, the terrible clashing bells are a nice touch, but by no means a formal opening. And so I have no trouble taking what would appear to be a step back: I find a pair of earbuds and pull up a Lustmord/White Ring darkwave-heavy playlist on my device. Time to settle in.

The careful reader (particularly one with an occult or ritualistic background) will note that no banishing, formal or otherwise, has occurred here. For what would be the point? The forces that will be called up can in no way be put down, and have always been present, and always will be. The idea that the speck of consciousness and will that I partake of could make any real claims to bind or otherwise restrict such forces is laughable. So why try? Banishing is a sucker move, performed by sucker MCs, and one of the first techniques of traditional magical practice the aspiring R'lyehian needs to drop from their experiential toolbox. I am not "performing" a ritual, not calling any corners, or otherwise setting up arbitrary parameters for a spiritual experience. I am diving *into* the experience.

The wind picks up. Over the drone in my headphones, I hear the yipping of a dog somewhere down the beach. Fires are being lit in clear patches between mangled driftwood architectures; it is the height of summer, after all, and there are humans about. I close my eyes and wait, watching nameless colours and strange, tangled geometries float against the back of my eyelids...

"Well, I gotta tell ya, I was expecting, like, carved basalt pillars or something..."

I laugh. It's my first guest, coming in to the spot from the left. It's now fully dark, and I can't make out his face, don't recognize the voice, and find I don't particularly care to know. Later I will learn his identity, but for now? For now, it doesn't matter. He's another mind, and I invite him to sit.

"Would it be all that much improved if there were?" I say.

"Ha. No. No, I'd say you'd be trying too hard. If there were."

"Exactly. Whiskey?"

"Oh, sure!" I hand him the bottle and he takes a drink. "Brought some wine, too. Little herb, if you're interested."

"Maybe later," I say. I am all for entheogenic enhancement of, oh, just about everything, but marijuana doesn't mesh well with the mindset I want to be in tonight.

"So, what are we doing here?" he asks.

"We are opening an etheric corridor to a R'lyehian ghetto."

"What does that mean?"

"It means sound came out of my mouth just now. It means we will be dreaming out loud. It means dogs will avoid this spot for weeks, and gulls will avoid flying through the air above it for months..."

"I suppose people will just walk right on through, though?"

I laugh again. "It's what we do, yeah. We receive. It means we will be concentrating the R'lyehian wavelength here, on this spot. This will be an outpost, so to speak." I wave a hand at the dark opening in the rock. "Maybe in that very pit. You should probably watch your feet."

"Nasty. OK, but what does all that *mean*?"

"It means *wait and see*."

And then we do, and while we wait, we drink and talk, and others arrive, one by one from out of the dark: a slight fellow in a long coat and scarves who I think might be a poet from an open mic I sometimes attend; a willowy, pixie-ish girl that my wife knows better than I do and who, frankly, I'm surprised to see, as she is perhaps typical of the sort of Left Coast second (third?) generation hippie that lives out here. We like her, though, so I'm glad to see her. It's going to be an interesting mix of minds.

Speaking of which, I begin to feel that always odd sensation as the demon (for lack of a better word) that has ridden me since that dream-filled week so many years ago settles in. Imagine a pulsating plane of light-that-is-not-light warping in from a direction that can't be pointed to and finally intersecting with the horizon line of your own vision. There is a shifting as my consciousness makes room for the altered awareness the demon brings. That, or leaves altogether, depending on the circumstances. My jaw begins to clench. I can feel staccato pops traveling up my spinal cord. A buzzing sound takes up residence in my left ear.

Fhtagn, I whisper to myself. Fhtagn.

(It's difficult to write about what occurred over the next several hours. Mostly because the "I" that normally moves through this world was barely present. And so that I now moves out of the present tense for the rest of this account, drawing what details there are from later discussions with the participants.)

I can recall asking those present to speak about their first exposure to Lovecraft, to his stories: which story? when? how did it affect them? and so on. Did the story augment or confirm or alter their beliefs at the time? We spoke of resonance, of deep archetypal functions, of that which for the most part remains unspoken and yet informs our actions in the world. Heady stuff, but nothing that couldn't be found in a philosophy coffee klatch down at your local hipster hangout.

What piqued my interest, and moved the conversation further out to sea (a completely appropriate term), effectively deepening the magical aspect of the night, was the revelation from the two males that their original exposure to R'lyehian themes had reached them through their dreams. Dreams that pre-dated their exposure to Lovecraft himself or his stories.

It was not until all present had related their histories that I revealed my own. The chittering up my spine had by this point become a steady thrum; the buzz in my left ear punctuated by sparks and hollow clacks as of bone being struck on bone. Everything was either awake or coming awake and the stars began to throb and spin in their velvet sockets. Speaking of those dreams (of that cliff, that ocean, that terrible rushing from beyond the western horizon) served to trigger the final synchronization between I and not-I; I'm told that the glossolalia began then. Mild at first, a low murmur of barbaric sound that before long evolved into extended sentences, consonant-heavy yowlings to beat the crashing of the waves, atonal dirges, ophidian slides into vocal registers I simply am unable to reproduce during normal consciousness[1].

At some point, I masked myself. Shaped leather, cold against my cheeks and pressing in on my temples, even as uncouth syllables continued to fly from my tongue like sparks. Those present felt compelled to use me then as oracle: dreams were related to the hybrid being I had become and interpretations were delivered back in halting, hissing English, though I was not aware of dropping back into my natal language. All language was of a piece to me. Everything was much of a muchness. Meaning rotted away for all, and we gazed on the bare white calcified scaffolding of our assumptions about Reality.

The whiskey was rapidly dwindling in the bottle, and the wine was already being passed around. The pothead began to smoke, and the pungent aroma mixed with the sharpness of the yellow cedar and benzoin in the smudge pots.

The pixie girl, becoming increasingly uncomfortable with the proceedings, spoke of the Earth and, perhaps predictably, referenced her dedication to Gaia. How quickly we invoke divine protectors. "What is a mother," I murmured, "if not the interface between that-which-is-not and that-which-is?

---

1   Later that night, as we retreated from the shore and moved through darkened parkland towards our beds, the poet produced from a pocket of his coat his own ragged paperback Ballantyne edition of Lovecraft and delivered this quote from *The Call of Cthulhu*...

"There are vocal qualities peculiar to men, and vocal qualities peculiar to beasts; and it is terrible to hear the one when the source should yield the other."

He then looked at me with a look that could only be described as significant.

A conduit into the world. A great passageway from formlessness into form. Mothers are to be feared."

"And loved," she countered.

"And loved," I agreed. "Both. Both, in all their terrible, perfect aspects..."

In that moment, the fractal branchings of Shub-Niggurath crackled into existence all about: driftwood snagged and banged on the rocks below us and the wind raked the Scotch broom on the cliff face behind us, sending up a dry rattle. The ghosts of all the mothers, stretching back through untold leagues of Time, sighing in assent.

The poet laughed nervously and shook himself violently. The pixie, now visibly restless, lit another smudge pot and murmured something about the chill.

"Iä, iä! Cthulhu fhtagn!" the poet cried. "In his house at R'lyeh, dead Cthulhu lies dreaming!" He stood then, a pale thin stick of a human at the edge of a world that could snuff him out in minutes, and cried out again. Behind the octopoid leather, the thing wearing the mask of my face twitched and pulled my lips into a grin and cried out as well. We all stood, the four of us... and yet more than four. All about we sensed shadow versions of ourselves, faint flickerings of alternate planes, other modes of being. Ghoul-selves, frog-selves, fish and lizard and armoured-insect selves. Aspects of life and form barely comprehensible: sentient equations, formulas that bred in the air and slipped worm-like between the stars. Membranes of quivering awareness, conscious mist, calculating mucks and oils: that old primordial slip-and-slide...

"And slimy things did walk with legs upon the slimy sea," recited the pothead.

We screamed and wept and gibbered in joy. There are times when a true gibbering session is just not cool. But not this time. We shouted and reveled and enjoyed ourselves. *All* of our selves. For we were Life, that abominable thing, the Thing That Should Not Be, and we[1] were on this beach at this moment calling out to the Lord of Dreams, of All That Is Not.

---

1 The destruction/multiplication of the so-called "core personality" that occurs during an event such as this is key to R'lyehian spirituality and attainment of the Black Gnosis. The royal "we", in this case, becomes an obvious choice when referring to oneself; it is, in fact, how I, or we, always think of ourselves. There are so many entities in here, after all. Obviously, we use the "I" when interacting with others, but this is for their comfort and convenience more than anything else. So, too, with the writing of this book. *When The Stars Are Right* by "Scott R Jones", indeed!

To say that the evening had become seriously profound is an understatement. Too profound, perhaps, for our pixie friend. As the fit of gibbering passed, she began to make sounds of distress and openly wondered if she should leave. "It's so dark out here," she said. "This is so dark. What are you *actually doing* here? There are things..."

"... best left alone?" finished the poet.

Of course, leaving alone the things best left alone is never the R'lyehian way. Does the wasp think about the possible consequences when it stings the larger beast? When we hesitate before looking into a mirror, do we truly know what gives us pause? The black scratchings of the channeled script glowed fiercely beneath the halogen spotlights and as I watched their writhings and listened to my companions, I felt a cold nausea rise in me. I tore the mask from my head and threw my sight into the thrumming dark between the reeling stars...

"I have seen the dark universe yawning," I recited, "where the black planets roll without aim. Where they roll in their horror unheeded, without knowledge, or luster, or name."

"Good Christ," the pixie whispered. Another divine protector invoked; the bright logic of the Sun, the warmth of compassion. "Fuck. Fucking hell, Scott."

"Where's that from?" the pothead asked.[1]

But I had no time to answer. The pixie was right, and her bald statement regarding things best left alone was as decent a cue as any for those very things to arrive. The corridor had opened. That which until a moment ago had been merely conceptual was now actual, and a howling began between our ears. There was now no distance between That Which Was and That Which Was Not: this chunk of rock was R'lyeh and R'lyeh was this chunk of rock. The stars, though not entirely right, had twisted out of their merely human alignment and the dark between them was a frothing, living thing, sentient and descending upon us.

I may have screamed. Certainly the others did: an unearthly sound, a mix of uncomprehending terror and fierce joy. I could not see the faces of the men, as they were turned from me and, like me, also looked to the writhing sky. In a chance moment, though, I caught the eyes of our pixie friend and saw true pain. Real psychic distress. I turned to her, took her hand in mine, put my mouth to her ear. There is a deep R'lyehian truth in the statement "Be just, and if you can't be just, be arbitrary."[2]

---

1 *Nemesis*, H.P. Lovecraft
2 William S Burroughs, as R'lyehian a character as there ever was.

She hadn't come prepared for any of this. And *that,* right there, is something that could be said about any of us, about *life.* So, to be subjected to the full force of the Black Gnosis would certainly constitute an arbitrary spasm of the true nature of the universe, I thought. Philosophically, I was aligned towards letting it happen for her... but then, the look in her eyes. I chose some small justice, instead. Later, she told me what I'd done...

"My son likes this lullaby," I said, as the ocean around us bloomed into phosphorescent spray. "Do you know that hobo ballad? *The Big Rock Candy Mountain?*"

"What? No."

I apparently sang the song in its entirety three times over, effectively creating a small pocket of warmth and whimsy that shielded her from the worst (or best?) of the shining obsidian energies that engulfed us. Cigarette trees and lemonade springs. Lakes of stew. Whiskey, too. Thoughts of my little boy, who she knew, being rocked to sleep in his dad's arms. What a gorgeous paradoxical feeling that must have been! To have the Big Rock Candy Mountains super-imposed over the churning non-Euclidean angles of R'lyeh![1] Layering her perceptions of me as a loving father and caring man over the demon-ridden spiritual entry point for an ultra-tellurian agency that I clearly also was! I have said elsewhere that the R'lyehian way, the way of the Black Gnosis, is a stealthy one, a profound practice of camouflage. That night, the pixie saw how such mimicry works.

She saw, and she survived. After the initial assault, the howling vibrations lessened to a steady, insect-chitter humming, and with the blessing of Shub-Niggurath, she thanked me and made her scrambling escape into the safer regions of the night, into the city and the houses of men. There was no circle to break, no wards to pass through; she simply left.

My remaining companions barely noticed her departure; on the heels of the corridor opening, a kind of fugue state had arrived. Conversation was barely coherent and comprised mostly of guttural barks, mumbled scraps of dream material, calls to the dead, and laughter. The latter became more and more pronounced as the night wore on: a bizarre kind of unfocussed hilarity that arose from no specific joke and went nowhere. Without origin and

---

1   For myself, I saw no contradiction: the Big Rock Candy Mountains, being an imaginal realm of archetypal vagabond delights, are of course contained within the infinite honeycombed dimensional lattice of that ur-City of Dream. Does not the sweet tang of some small pleasure render a nightmare all the more transcendent? In its House in R'lyeh, dead Cthulhu waits dreaming, and its House has many rooms.

having no target, The Grin[1] was upon us, and before long we were doubled over in a fit of madness-induced mirth.

This passed as well, and a silence fell, a silence that became more and more profound as the minutes ticked by. With it came the sensation of amazing pressure, of an atmosphere becoming more dense with each intake of breath. The rock was sinking. The pit, filling up from below. The sea, rising.

"Time to leave," I whispered. The corridor was opened, *we* were opened, and this place belonged to R'lyeh now. There was a delicious panic rising in my chest and I hurried to pack the tools and gear. The others helped as well: I ordered the pages of script to be torn to shreds and given to the wind, the last of the alcohol poured out on the rocks.

"For our deep down homies!" the poet shrieked.

As the others scrambled across the rocks and tide-tossed deadwood toward the cliff, I took up the mask in my hands, placed my lips to the cold, ridged leather of the forehead, and arranged it on a large stone near the lip of the pit. I had not planned to sacrifice it, to leave it there as tribute for whatever would come for it (the thing was ridiculously expensive, for what it was, and had served me well for years; parting with it was sheer idiocy), but in the moment it made utter sense. I was not in my right mind when I did it; nevertheless, it was *right* to do so. In these things, I trust my demon, trust the moment. Perhaps I was making up, in some small way, for letting the pixie get away.

Not that anyone really *does* with a thing like this. R'lyeh rises in every human heart, and if, for untold reasons, the city did not breach the surface of her awareness this night, it would later.

We climbed to the top of the cliff and went our separate ways. Lone men in the dark, shambling through shadowed parks and alleyways, spewing curses and spontaneous poetry and sobs, on our way to beds and notebooks and fevered dreams. Waiting, reluctant, for daylight and the return of rational thought.

Fhtagn.

---

1   One of the marks of the R'lyehian, see the chapter *The Black Gnosis.*

My Own Private Necronomicon

Bring something incomprehensible into the world!
— Gilles Deleuze, *A Thousand Plateaus:*
Capitalism and Schizophrenia

There was a time when Lovecraft's fabled tome of eldritch horror, the *Necronomicon*, enjoyed an existence as a purely fictional construction: a prop device to generate shudders, cleverly propped up itself by Lovecraft's cheeky placement of it on a bookshelf lined with actual historical volumes. There it sat, rare and imaginary, mouldering away right next to *De Vermis Mysteriis* and the *Pnakotic Manuscripts*, book ended by Miss Margaret Murray's *The Witch Cult in Eastern* Europe and Frazier's *The Golden Bough*[1].

That time ended the moment some naïve but enterprising reader of *Weird Tales* thought to enquire of his local librarian why the *Necronomicon* was not listed in the card catalogue.

Since that moment, the *Necronomicon* and its legend has grown and continues to grow. Lovecraft himself wrote a brief, tongue-in-cheek monograph on its black history[2] but of course, the fabrications did not stop there. In the years since its first appearance in Lovecraft's short tale *The Hound* in 1924, the *idea* of the book has spawned any number of hoax texts[3] and blatantly commercial attempts to cash in on the books' notoriety. One of

---

1 *De Vermis Mysteriis* and the *Pnakotic Manuscripts*, of course, also being fictional, the creations of Robert Bloch and Lovecraft, respectively. Murray's book is quite real, though, as is Frazier's.

2 *History of the Necronomicon*, H. P. Lovecraft (written in 1927 but only published after his death in 1938).

3 If I can be said to have a favourite of these at all, then surely it is the scholarly reserve of George Hay and Colin Wilson's 1978 *The Book of Dead Names*, which, loaded with magic square ciphers, the then-still-mysterious *Voynich Manuscript*, and a masterful "translation" of the text by occultist Robert Turner, is a deliciously dry yet unsettling work. I'm convinced Lovecraft would have approved of Hay and Wilson's effort above all others.

these, the *Simon Necronomicon* (or *Simonomicon*, as it is sometimes called; a cobbled-together source-book of Sumerian magical spells with a thin candy Mythos shell), has never gone out of print since its first cheap paperback run and has sold *over 800,000 copies worldwide*, not including the several volumes of workbooks and commentaries associated with it. As a book of diabolical magic, the *Simonomicon* is subpar, but as a publishing success it is unparalleled.

As with the indescribable things found between its blood-and-ichor stained covers, the *Necronomicon* is a book best left in the realm of the idea if it is to be at all effective. Time and again it's been pointed out that the *Necronomicon* works best (as a prop, perhaps even as a hoax) when the bulk of it remains untranslated, un-actualized. Unreal. The late UK occultist Kenneth Grant played upon this quality of the book in a clever work-around *vis a vis* its authenticity: the *Necronomicon* is an astral book according to Grant, existing as a kind of fog-of-potential in the Akashic records, accessed through focused magical work, dream recording, hypnosis and what-have-you. Using these techniques, portions of the book could be *transcribed,* brought down (through? across?) to our world.

Of course, the danger here is the same as with most, if not all, of the channeling efforts that characterize the New Age plague[1]: whatever wisdom that may be obtained from spirits or ultra-telluric entities from beyond will, according to the very nature of the transmission, be contaminated by the receiver. Of *course* it's a good idea to eat your wheat germ and be kind to your neighbour, envisioning positivity while cleansing your chakras... but you didn't need an angel or alien or some hybrid angelien to tell you that, using your own tongue, now, did you? Most channeled wisdom is comprised of merely good advice, common-sense things that everybody knows already, passed through a filter of higher spiritual authority for easier digestibility.

The same goes for the dark magics and maddening revelations of the *Necronomicon* (astral edition): anything a human mind could pull from its etheric bulk would naturally arrive tainted, not with TrueEvil™ (usually the first and laughably human goal of would-be latter-day Alhazreds) or even with Madness, but with the worst contamination of all...

Comprehensibility.

From Lovecraft on, the *Necronomicon* (in all its hokey or scholarly or pseudo-Crowleyan incarnations) has universally been regarded as the prime textual source of the Black Gnosis. All (from hack horror writers to movie

---

1 Which, here on the far side of the thoroughly uneventful date of December 21 2012, we are now, as a culture, finally starting to get over. I hope.

directors to Lovecraft scholars) agree that this is a book which can drive a reader insane. A dangerous book. A banned and blasphemous and flame-worthy book. This fictional, imaginary, made-up book. This *Al Azif*. This "howling of the demon-insects in the wind of the desert".

Comprehensibility will always be the uniquely human curse that leaves the *Necronomicon* firmly on the astral plane. It will never be checked out of the Akashic records, to be brought screaming and gnashing its teeth[1] into the library of some very unlucky cultist.

That being said, the problem does present the R'lyehian with an interesting challenge, one that should be taken up by every serious seeker of the Black Gnosis: the *Necronomicon*, like R'lyeh, must be raised. The R'lyehian must claim *authorship* of their own personal copy. What does this mean and what will the book look like once it is completed?[2]

Above all other considerations, the privately penned *Necronomicon* of the R'lyehian seeker[3] must be a channel for the Black Gnosis. It must be *utterly baffling*. If it begins to read like a common spell book or pagan Book of Shadows, then it is already a lost cause. Sadly, most attempts to create the *Necronomicon* fall in the very centre of this category, and despite the great effort and clear artistic talent applied to their creation, these books are merely novelties: picture books with cramped blackletter text, movie props, vehicles for adolescent power fantasies[4].

In fact, if the thing can be read at all, it is already a failure. The *Necronomicon* should, ideally, be an asemic text for all readers, and if possible, for the author as well: word or word-like structures that provide a conceptual cage, a lattice-work of line and form, and behind the lattice, barely

---

1 I direct you to the flapping puppet-on-a-string version of the *Necronomicon* from Sam Raimi's classic 1992 film *Army of Darkness*. I know you went there. You know I know, too.

2 Knowing in advance that with a fractal tome such as this, living and breathing as it does in the shadow of Borges, there is no such thing as a "completed" *Necronomicon*: it's pages are infinite, there is no middle page.

3 It's a personal choice, but perhaps the book in question is less the *Necronomicon* and more properly the *R'lyeh Text*. Better still, it is the "nameless tome" of the stories and of the dreams of all men. For our purposes here, though, the *Necronomicon* (as a catch-all title for weird and dangerous books everywhere) will suffice.

4 A simple test for the authenticity of your DIY *Necronomicon*: imagine that you are entertaining guests, and, due to a blasphemous lack of discretion, your book is left out on the coffee table for all to see. If anyone says "What's this? The *Necronomicon*?" then the book fails the test. Remember that the R'lyehian way is one of stealth and camouflage, and, in the case of the holy book, incomprehensibility. Uneasy feelings around the book are fine, but outright amused recognition is not, for it is the surest sign of the hobbyist, the pastiche-artist, the dilettante.

concealed by this lace of wordless wordings, seethes the Black Gnosis, operating on the reader in a trans-linguistic fashion. Comprehended, yes, but not through the act of reading. There is meaning there, but it is a meaning that is delivered to the hollow spaces in the individual, to That Which Is Not within them. The text comes from Void and is naturally called to Void. While viewing the text, the reader should experience the disquieting sensation that they themselves are the one being read by the book, that interacting with the pages is not a one-way operation. The urge to suddenly twist around to look over your shoulder should be strong during any contemplation of the pages.

As such, the *Necronomicon* should *feel dangerous*. If our reaction to a personal edition of the book is a chuckle or a bemused, mocking (or even admiring) appraisal of its contents, then it is useless for R'lyehian purposes. That being said, the chance to have a reaction to a private *Necronomicon* should never actually come to the casual reader: this is a book that must be kept under lock and key. Hidden. A dark treasure. It is not a volume to be shared, or gloated over, or displayed openly on lectern, bookshelf or coffee table.

So, a book that is primarily asemic (untainted by semantic content), largely unseen, opening into and onto the Black Gnosis as experienced personally and transcribed by the R'lyehian author: but what, after all, are the *actual contents* of the *Necronomicon*? This will vary according to the individual, but some or all of the following are possibilities...

Records of alternate histories. Personal fetishes: sexual and otherwise. Dreams[1]. Overheard scraps of the speech of the Great Old Ones as they murmur in their immemorial sleep. Visions. Poetic or anti-poetic description of the paths of the stars through the void. Transcriptions of the susurrus that moves between the earth and the low cloud that comes off the sea in the early dawn hours. Spectral dialogues. Yes, even that same howling of the demon-insects in the wind of the desert. The hum of your city, your building, your dormant machines at three in the morning. Random samplings of random books from random bookshelves run through a random code generator. Random media feeds[2]. Memories of the future.

As for illustrations, if the R'lyehian is skilled with pen and ink, charcoal, or conté crayon[3], then certainly attempts should be made to augment the

---

1 The author needs to exercise care, here. The *Necronomicon* should never devolve into a mere dream journal.

2 In generating this kind of document, the cut-up techniques of Brian Gysin and William Burroughs are always useful and surprisingly forgiving.

3 Or, indeed, other, less mentionable media. Ask any decent working ceremonial magician: the *frisson* of working with life fluids never goes away. This is, after all, a book of madness: to pen the entire thing without once descending there with pen

text with appropriate graphics. If the R'lyehian is not skilled, then collage is another excellent option. And again, as with the text, the author will need to be careful with any depictions of the Great Old Ones, angle-webs and diagrams, or the trappings of magical practice: things that will mark the book as a juvenile work. These are best left in the realm of the abstract symbol, the wash of particular colours on the page in certain combinations, the smell of the author's sweat where it has stained the paper.

The breath that moves through all of the above must have one source and one goal: the Black Gnosis. If the text does not derive from that source, it must at least be a genuine attempt to dive towards it; a hyper-ventilation in written form, preparing the mind for increasingly courageous drops into the pressured depths of R'lyeh.

The *Necronomicon* of the R'lyehian, then, is simply this: a meditation tool, both in its creation and in its contemplation. It is a reflection of the movement of his psyche as it mutates and adapts to the R'lyehian environment, tracking the movement of the stars within him as they come round again in the cycle of eternity. It is a vehicle, a craft for sailing and plumbing the dark seas of infinity that surround our placid island of ignorance. It is the work of decades, a lifetime, and it is precious, unique in all the world. No other R'lyehian can write your *Necronomicon*.

It begins with a single stroke of the pen, but who can say where it may end?

---

in hand is to invite failure, and the letting out of a little of your own crimson is as swift a road as any to that state. If anything, it signals to your conscious mind that *things are serious now.*

The Wisdom in the Clay

I can recall a time (and this not so long ago, not really) when the only Lovecraft-inspired artwork one could find, in print or on the internet, was old Weird Tales magazine covers, the illustrations and paintings commissioned by Sandy Petersen for his *Call of Cthulhu* role-playing game materials, and of course the cover artwork for the Arkham House editions of Lovecraft's collected works. In particular, the cover painting for the corrected sixth edition of *The Dunwich Horror and Others*, executed with subtle grace by Raymond Bayless (portraying a rather subdued and even poised Cthulhu emerging from its tomb, a sailor pinched delicately between thumb and forefinger), was practically ubiquitous for years, being the first result of any search for Cthulhu, the image slowly filling the monitor line by line, as a modem chittered away in a frenzy of white noise and data.

Over the past decade, this situation has changed considerably. There are now so many artists and craftspersons working near to or within the Lovecraftian *milieu*, that one could easily spend months viewing it all. From pulpy comic-book style renderings through to intricate digital masterpieces and sculpture in all mediums, the Great Old Ones have captured the imaginations of artists across the planet. What drives an artist towards Lovecraft's imagery? To attempt to describe, using paint and pixel, the indescribable?

On the face of it, we can be sure that the attraction is a basic one: people love to draw monsters, and Lovecraft's extra-dimensional, multi-limbed, amorphous beasties provide plenty of fodder for the cavalcade of horrors that can now be accessed by anyone. Delving deeper into the question, though, we may find more subversive energies at work, energies that point to a space that lies beyond the genuine creative kick of monster-making. Energies which may be clarified with another question: what qualities separate the artists who use the Great Old Ones as simple templates, and those who could be thought of as working in (if I may be so bold as to suggest it) a R'lyehian tradition, or movement? Where may we split the merely grotesque from the gnostic? The crass from the cosmic, the commercial from the compelling?

We can begin by removing from our consideration the vast bulk of material produced with tongue obviously in cheek: the smirking Cthulhu t-shirts, the mash-ups of Lovecraftian deities with popular brands and entertainment properties, the cutesy renderings[1] of Great Old Ones wearing clothes or working in an office cubicle or wearing funny hats, and of course, atop this mountain of misunderstanding and sugar, the felt-and-stuffing abomination that is the glass-eyed Plush Cthulhu, in its many, many forms[2]. Barely art and most certainly product, designed and marketed solely to tease a buck out of a tiny, specialized sliver of the consumer horde...

"Dude! Check it out. I am rocking the eldritch tee today!"

"Fhtagn! Sweet tentacles[3], brah!"

1   Along with the popular kai-ju representations of the Great Old Ones (Cthulhu in particular) the saccharine dreck produced by purveyors of this "Hello Kitty"-ing of the Mythos gods is truly lamentable. Japan has a *lot* to answer for in this regard.

2   The merest glance at a toy website reveals a staggering array of plushness: Blue Velvet Cthulhu, Santa Claus Cthulhu, *Mini* Santa Claus Cthulhu, Electronic Screaming Cthulhu (presumably equipped with some type of soundbox in its bean-filled tummy), a silver-and-black Goth Cthulhu (as distinct from the orange-and-black Hallow's Eve Cthulhu), Miskatonic University Graduate Cthulhu with mortarboard and degree, Secret Agent Cthulhu, Summer Fun Cthulhu, Superhero Cthulhu, and finally an all-red Valentino Cthulhu.

Summer Fun Cthulhu.

3   It *should* go without saying, but sadly does not, that the depiction of tentacles does not a Lovecraftian artwork make, and this is even more so when considering R'lyehian art. As mentioned in the introduction to this book, the Tentacle has become the graphic sign of Evil in the 21st Century, and this largely due to Lovecraft's influence, or rather, the influence of the tastemakers who craft our popular entertainments. Some of these creators are very open about their affection for the Mythos (the film director Guillermo del Toro being a prime example) and their skill in presenting Mythos themes and monsters is contagious. So much so that things are being branded "Mythos" and "Lovecraftian" that are not, in fact, anywhere near such territory.

An example. At the time of this writing, I have received in my email inbox and through social media sites, dozens of *Cthulhu-pies*: a photograph of a fruit pie (some dark berry, or perhaps strawberry-rhubarb; the resolution of this photo is not great, so it can be hard to tell) with a crust cleverly made into the image of a scowling octopoid face with flaky tentacles flailing. Sometimes there is a groan-worthy caption ("Is this a new pie? No, it is an Old One") and sometimes not. The friends and acquaintances who forward this thing to me are all well-intentioned and even excited to be able to share in the fun of it, and while I admit the pie looks tasty, I will confess here that *I am so very sick of seeing this thing*. Now, if someone will bake me the Cthulhu-pie, I will enjoy it thoroughly and *fhtagn* along with all present,

Yes, sweet. Sweetness we can readily leave behind in our search, which now takes us into the realm of the horror artist, a territory where Lovecraft himself, he who created the character of Richard Upton Pickman[1], would feel quite at home. It is here we will find surreal landscapes worthy of Bosch, tortured flesh, gruesome scenes of every kind. There is blood here and agonies undreamed of, in shunned houses and upon blasted heaths and atop withering crags. Here the Great Old Ones, or more often their servants, stir from slumber to move and mock and murder.

It is here, too, where we run screaming from what I've come to call the *kaiju problem*[2] in Mythos art. This is the seemingly irresistible compulsion to depict the moment when the stars come right as a standard-issue apocalypse of the Biblical type, where the physical destruction of cities, landscapes, and human populations takes precedence. In these tableaus we are restricted to the viewpoint we are already quite used to: that of the human, looking up from the ground, and usually within our last seconds of gibbering life. While this may hold a certain *frisson* for the viewer, it fails to address the essential shift in Reality itself that would be the truly defining characteristic of the Great Old One's return[3].

Which is to say, ending the world is all well and good, but changing it completely, swapping it out for something new, incomprehensibly beautiful and maddening, and, yes, better? That takes work. That is the work of gods, and who can know how that work is accomplished or how it looks as it is being done? We imagine destruction, for that is all we can imagine or are suited to imagine, and, like Lovecraft himself, we imagine the return of the

---

because despite how I may come across in these pages, I am not without a sense of humour regarding the R'lyehian spiritual path, but friends! Friends, it is not Cthulhu. It is only an angry octopus. It is not even an octopus.

It is a *pie*.

1   the titular artist of the story *Pickman's Model*

2   Briefly touched upon in the chapter *On Cthulhu*.

3   I need only direct the reader to the cover illustration of the Mythos fiction anthology *Cthulhu Unbound 3* (Permuted Press) to clarify this point. A spectacular piece of art by Peter Fussey, it depicts Great Cthulhu itself, risen, finally, and engaging in predictably one-sided battle with an aircraft carrier and several fighter jets: the planes that are not actually on fire soon will be, and the carrier itself is grasped in one of Cthulhu's titan paws. A dire situation, clearly, and yet the R'lyehian *must* ask: how are the men and women piloting and sailing those machines *sane enough to do so*? Madness made flesh has risen from the depths to claim its rightful dominion against upstart mankind and somehow we manage to keep it together long enough to get a carrier group into the South Pacific? Like any fantasy, it strains credulity.

Great Old Ones as a baptism of fire, as the ravening of monsters across a planet laid waste.

Granted, a ravening it very well may be, but the R'lyehian sees beyond such depictions to the reality (*R'lyehity?*) behind the divine actions of her gods. And what is that reality?

Whatever else it may be on the surface, it is *primal* at the core. It is *serene*. Undimensioned and unseen. Eternal and unchanging. The Great Old Ones were, are, and shall be. Their existence is the natural order of things, and that order is Chaos, which is to say the original undifferentiated oneness of all things. The Black Gnosis made solid.

With these qualities in mind, the task of picking out artists working in the R'lyehian tradition becomes simplicity itself. Personal taste will be a factor in our selections, naturally, but in all of these there will be found a potent essence of *primal serenity*, of the still abysses of Deep Time, of quiet yet unthinkable power and Madness held and nurtured so long and under such pressures that it has become almost indistinguishable from peace. I say *almost*, because by its very nature, the Madness of the Old Ones is liable to break out at any moment to consume the consumer of the art. There should be a near unbearable tension to the work, something, some urge to look that keeps the eye lingering longer than it normally would. And if that urge is examined closely, it is found to stem from a vague unease that, should we look away, the Thing in the Painting will move, and in that moving our fate decided.

R'lyehian art, then, is powerful yet poised. Quiet and disquieting. Fresh in its newness, in the novelty of its portrayals of ancient, timeless things and beings. It is meditative and yet it unsettles. The human quails before it even as it stirs the R'lyehian soul, mirrors the shifting of vast continents of feeling and perception deep beneath the surface of the psyche. As Jean-Luc Goddard said, art attracts us only by what it reveals of our most secret self... and the R'lyehian is *all about that secret self.*

In the end, perhaps the best test of whether a piece of Lovecraftian art is in the genuine R'lyehian tradition is akin to the classic line "I don't know much about art, but I know what I like". To wit: does the piece trigger a bemused chuckle... or a sharp intake of awed breath which catches in the throat? Does it inspire the words "cool, but I've seen it before"... or the silent, surprised recognition of something never seen which is still, somehow, utterly familiar, as a vision from a half-remembered dream?

Visions, trance, strange altered states of consciousness, dreams: it is these surreal territories from which R'lyehian art should flow and it is these that it fuels. And though the R'lyehian may view such art and feel its pull, its primal gravity, viewing it pales in comparison to the act of creation itself.

Not all R'lyehians can *be* artists, of course. Sculpture, painting, illustration, digital manipulation, music, film: these are skills that can and should take years to develop. Those fortunate enough to possess raw talent still require refinement of that talent. We are not all so blessed. But this does not mean that the R'lyehian should shy away from artistic production.

For it is in the creative act that the R'lyehian is able to shift his consciousness away from the human world. Yes, there is a horror in the clay, but also a wisdom: artistic labour, in any medium, affords the artist a deep, self-less focus on the Things That Are Not, even as those things are brought into the Real. Each piece in its creation is a meditative doorway. And once completed (whether the work of a hundred hours on canvas and drawing tablet, or the work of an hour with clay and stone), the piece becomes a talisman. It creates a kind of psychic weight which pulls the mind of the R'lyehian down to R'lyeh. It becomes a locus for the Black Gnosis, drawing the divine madness to itself in ever-increasing layers of dense atmosphere.

What do humans make? Pretty things or useless things. Narcissistic things. *Comprehensible* things. The R'lyehian attempts to make Things That Should Not Be. Things from Outside. The Art of the Abyss, of the Gulf, of the Void.

Of course, we fail. I fail in this all the time. I am a better writer than an artist, and I am a poor artist indeed: my only output consists of a kind of Islamic-calligraphy-inspired portraiture, using the cursives and acute angles of the channeled script to form shapes on the page. At their best, my sketches are barely warmed-over pastiche of Austin Osman Spare, and most are discarded.

Once a year, though, I make an attempt at sculpture, in clay or soapstone. Always the subject is Cthulhu. And once a year, I produce a passable representation. Sometimes I opt for the classic posture: squatting atop a pedestal, dormant, bloated, wings folded behind. Other years I have put Cthulhu in lotus posture, clean-limbed and smooth, hands positioned in R'lyehian mudras. Cthulhu's visage I have worked to be monstrous, calm, enraged, noble, reserved, beatific. Some sculptures have taken a month or more to create; others are the work of an evening, rough-hewn and primitive. In many ways, I like these best.

In all cases, once created, these eidolons rest for a time on bookshelf or table in my working space, the focus of occasional meditations and repetitions of the Cthulhusattva Vow. Then (and who can say what triggers this moment?) they are removed from my spaces, sometimes destroyed, reduced to fragments and dust, and other times relocated to rocky alcoves at the shoreline, interred in the rotting cores of old growth trees, placed in shadowed openings in the crumbling brickwork of a forgotten alleyway.

"It is new, indeed," (says the sculptor Wilcox of a bas-relief, in Lovecraft's *The Call of Cthulhu*) "for I made it last night in a dream of strange cities; and dreams are older than brooding Tyre, or the contemplative Sphinx, or garden-girdled Babylon."

Yes, art, like the dreams from which it is born, comes from the unconscious and, if it is pure art, returns there loaded with new import, fresh insights into the condition of both art and artist. I entertain no illusions, here: my sculptures are amateurish at best, my illustrations merely satisfactory. I press on with them all the same, for their redeeming feature is not their outward quality, but the mental state I enter into during their creation, and for a time afterward. Molding the eidolon of Cthulhu, my fingers cold with wet clay or blistered and dust-caked from working a file over a soapstone block, I meditate on the form of Madness, the rough lineaments of Dream. I enter into an almost physical rapport with the Lord of Dreams, and, though my skills are yet rudimentary, I can at certain moments recognize that feeling, expressed by more talented artists than I, of the subject of the work already present in the stone and waiting for release. It is meditative action, this art-making. Devotional, humbling, and a supreme ego-lytic tool.

R'lyehian art surfaces from below, and it is returned there as well. I destroy my work in order to atomize it, cast it upon the winds or the water: a form has had its moment, solidified in Time, and is then released, carrying with it the memory of a past shape. The pieces that remain intact but are sent out into the world serve the same function. They are lost to me. They will weather away and most will never be found, but their presence in natural space or urban environment creates pockets of Black Gnosis, temporary autonomous altars to the Incomprehensible.

Destruction and secret distribution are my own preferred methods of performing this priestly service. Perhaps if my skills were of a higher grade, I would lose (and loose) my work to the world by another method: by keeping it intact, displaying it for others to see. Consider the proliferation of Lovecraftian imagery over the last ten years. Ponder the significance of artists worldwide creating R'lyehian art in such quantity that to wade through it all would be near impossible. If each piece of art is a conceptual entry-point into R'lyehian awareness, each drawing a door, each sculpture a doorstop, then the flood of Cthulhu-inspired imagery[1] in these days is surely indicative of strange stirrings in the blackness beneath our culture.

---

1   A simple test of this can be performed: show random persons a decent depiction of Cthulhu and keep track of how many recognize the Lord of Dreams.

The Black Gnosis *is* rising. Slowly, to be sure, but it is there, peering out from computer screen and movie screen alike, from sketchbook and canvas, from the flaming depths of the kiln and the dry rustle of the comic book. As the stars come right, even the unregenerate and ignorant feel the changes that are soon to be brought down upon the world.

The R'lyehian feels them, too, in the clay, on the page, and in her own hands as they mold that clay and mark that page, and she knows it for a great wisdom. So, make art, for your own pleasure and enlightenment foremost, and later for the enjoyment and insight it may bring to others.

You'll find that a surprisingly large percentage of those polled *will know* who they're looking at. At the same time, ask the positive responders whether they have read any Lovecraft, or even know of Lovecraft. An interesting disparity is sure to arise. These are strange times.

The Unbearable Strangeness of Being:
Sex and the R'lyehian

Life is played out on many stages, and surely one of the larger, more luridly lit and multi-tiered of these is the one labeled *Sex[1]*. The painted backdrop against which our sexual lives are thrown in contrast is of course Death (as is the final curtain rung down on all our stages): knowledge, or even suspicion, of our last moments only adds to the piquant nature of those earlier moments in which we rail against our eventual cessation as beings.

It is these two drives in us, towards Sex and away from Death (though this is sometimes reversed, or simultaneously experienced, even), twinned and antagonistic and misunderstood as they are, that are also the root cause of much of our suffering as a species. We rush, all brainless and instinctual, towards the connection of Sex from the moment we learn that such a thing exists, and we cringe in uncomprehending fear from the consummation of Death, fleeing the full knowledge of its mysteries.

For the R'lyehian, the sexual act, in all its varied forms, is not only performed in pursuit of pleasure, it is performed in the pursuit of the Black Gnosis. Recall that the third attribute of the Black Gnosis is the *Burning Gaze*: the lust for connection and knowledge and experience that typifies the R'lyehian world-view. And though pleasure (and to a lesser extent for those given to it, procreation) can be said to be the main goals of sexual

---

1   Also the one with the biggest prop budget.

union, the practicing R'lyehian enters into it with a view to something more, namely, the cultivation of their personal *tantra* of the strange, the unfathomable, and the weird.

Sex is weird. Let's be honest here: when you get right down into the squelchy, heaving, multi-limbed mass of the thing, sex is very weird indeed. Sex is weird, because just *being* is weird. The fact that we are conscious entities parading around in flesh, flesh that occasionally comes together to please itself and, when conditions are right, produce more flesh for other conscious entities to parade around in? Completely weird.

Most of the time, we simply don't notice how odd this is, how utterly strange our existence as a species on this planet has become. We are long past the simple days of our animal bruting-about, and each moment we are engaging more and more with the thing that we are to become. For now, we are strange, soft, pulpy creatures moving about the surface of this rock in our rags and silks and armours, cloaked in ideas and studded over with glowing memes, parasitical hoardings of belief and faith, ignorance and obsession. Can we truly claim that our behaviours, our proclivities and preferences, are even our own? Our society itself, an epiphenomenal entity sprouting from the fevered bios of its fleshy host if ever there was one, has its own obsessions. In regards to sex, society's primary obsession is with normative behaviour, and this is a symptom of that not-noticing, that willful ignorance of the outré nature of the human experiment. Of the life experiment.

Sex sells and is sold. Ecstasy and anxiety are its products. It cages even as it frees. Look to the multitude of labels given to gender expression, sexual preference, and lifestyle choice: we are given to understand that the current LGBQT-MNOP alphabet soup of possible roles and modes of sexual being is a progressive movement, a real step forward. And yet this proliferation of labels, each with their staunch and strident defenders and detractors, has contributed little towards any reasonable increase in sexual freedom, and resulted in no real decrease in the level of sexual anxiety in our increasingly fractured society. Labels are for the marketplace, and the marketplace is primarily concerned with cost, supply, demand, brand loyalty, and the act of consuming. Each brand merely serves to define what it is not: by their very existence they shore up and validate the sexualities they set themselves against, reinforcing the standardized behaviours of every other brand. Sexual ghettos are the result, cages in which individuals imagine themselves free.

The R'lyehian, then, sees through this commodification of our sexual nature, to the inherent Being-Strangeness at the core of our existence, and the attendant weird-tantra of the sexual act as an expression of that strangeness. Labels and gender roles flow from the R'lyehian's skin like water: though they may enjoy and even prefer a primary sexual orientation (heterosexual, homosexual, bi-, queer, and yes, even asexual[1]), they are not fixed there, pinned to the board like a common moth to be gawked at and then forgotten. The R'lyehian way is, again, one of camouflage and stealth, and so, as far as sex is concerned, the R'lyehian is, at her core, an *omni-sexual being*.

The R'lyehian strives to point the way to the sex-practices of the future, to the foretold "holocaust of ecstasy and freedom" that will be the hallmark of that day when the stars are right. Omni-sexual R'lyehian practice recalls the Sufi's ecstatic connection to something as basic and simple as, say, a glass of water. The R'lyehian is drunk on significance, aroused by the *import* of things before anything else. Beyond mere fetish attachment[2], the omni-sexual R'lyehian is turned on by conceptual items, ideas of transcendence, mutation, severe body modifications. Omni-sexuality is transhumanist and transformative. Transformation through sex, and sex with whoever and whatever will trigger such transformation[3].

The R'lyehian, already well familiar with the Abyss and that which gazes from within it, having received the Wink from that dread "I" and welcomed

---

1 In truth, ones preference here is an entirely surface presentation, as much a stealth cloak as the so-called personality: all modes of sexual expression are open to the R'lyehian and can and should be accessed at any time, should the situation call for it. That being said, the R'lyehian is not "in the closet", so to speak, or, if they are, that closet is *effectively infinite*, and the multitude of personalities, ideations, and modes of sexual gratification within it are similarly endless. The R'lyehian is a thousand white-hot compartments. He makes no judgments regarding the modes of being within himself (the very definition of a Sisyphean task!) and extends that openness outwards to others as well. If there is a criteria of judgment at all *vis a vis* R'lyehian omni-sexual practice, it comes down to one thing: the bare wiring of the nervous system. To wit: all beings, if they are wired up at all, move towards pleasure and away from pain (a basic polymorphic approach), and the means by which this pleasure is attained is inconsequential, merely epiphenomenal. As far as the R'lyehian is concerned, sex is whatever turns you on, and this *literally* so. The wires must fire.

2 Developing fetish attachments is a dead end for the R'lyehian. Following the plastic and temporary nature of her personality matrices, her varied cloaks and armours and shells, why would she lock down her ability to derive omni-sexual pleasure from anything into a fetish? Literally, *one* thing: artificial and manufactured in the Latin sense.

3 It should go without saying, but sadly does not, that this grouping does not include children. The practicing, conscientious R'lyehian would not attempt to bring an unformed, immature human mind into contact with the Black Gnosis, for obvious reasons; neither would they engage in any kind of sexual activity with underage persons for any reason.

the Black Gnosis into his life, seeks to train his Burning Gaze upon the ebon depths and make love to the Abyss itself. He remembers that there is a hole in Everything (and this no more so than within himself), and seeks to fill it. The Abyss, the concourses and catacombs and chambers of R'lyeh: these are the honeycombed voids in which the self may be lost. And what is the definition of ecstasy, if it is not loss of self? Who would not take any route, *many* routes, as many as possible, toward that union with That Which Is Not?

The R'lyehian approaches reality itself as a breeding medium, one with which he is constantly engaged in intercourse: everything he touches must take on his distinctive taint. The multiplicity of incarnation via Yog-Sothoth, the sheer exuberance embodied in the fecundity of Shub-Niggurath, the self-destroying heat of Nyarlathotep's conflagration of meaning/not-meaning: all these contribute to the raising of R'lyeh in the R'lyehian's heart, soul, and bedroom. The Black Gnosis may be triggered in the moment of orgasm, or at any moment during the sexual act (or indeed at *any moment at all,* sexual or otherwise) by allowing the Being-Strangeness of the act itself manifest fully in the consciousness. This awareness is brought forth through a meditation on fear.

Why do we enter into sex with such abandon? The classical figures of Death and the Maiden provide some small clue. Despite our knowledge of Shub-Niggurath's might as the Conqueror Womb, the destroyer of Time and Death, that fear of our individual dissolution as embodied entities rides us strong, and rides us straight into the arms of our casual sexual partners, our lovers, our life-long mates. Fear drives us, for, as Lovecraft was fond of pointing out, it is the oldest and strongest of our emotions.

The R'lyehian, in allowing herself to become aware of that fear which is at the root of the sexual act *during* the act itself, may steer the experience towards an outbreak of the Black Gnosis. The moment of orgasm becomes a one-pointed awareness, the clear ringing of a single sunken bell in the deep. In the middle of the vast Pacific of her own pleasure, a single coordinate pings its location: 47° 9' S 126° 43' W. And from those pressured depths, Madness arises, with Ecstasy in tow. She is the water and the wave, and experiences the Chill, the Grin, and the Burning Gaze of the Black Gnosis simultaneously.

All things considered, it is likely wise that the R'lyehian's sexual partner be, if not R'lyehian themselves, at the least philosophically aligned with the rudiments of R'lyehian thought, for the intensity of sharing, even in a partial sense, in the ecstasy of a sexually generated eruption of the Black Gnosis could be highly disturbing to the uninitiated. For our purposes here, the term "fucking frightening" would not be an inappropriate descriptor of the experience. Like any decent *tantra,* the R'lyehian sex-practice is best when fully shared between partners: there is no cloistering of oneself within a private experience, using the other person[1] merely as a tool applied to the creation of our own pleasure. If the Black Gnosis is triggered, then it is transmitted, through the eyes and skin, the fingers and teeth and musculature. If it is to be at all effective, then it is *shared,* and that sharing can profoundly disturb the mind of the unprepared partner.

Naturally, preparing a partner for the psychic rigours of R'lyehian sex practice is entirely up to the individual. Such preparations could range anywhere from a simple "this might get weird" to lengthy periods of exposure to the Black Gnosis as the R'lyehian experiences them in his day to day life. For our part, we (and indeed, most potential partners) appreciate the simple approach, as there is very little need to belabour the point: in common parlance, R'lyehian sex "is what it is" and like most things of that ilk, it is better to experience it than be merely lectured at about it. If it becomes something that the non-R'lyehian enjoys, for their own reasons, then all the better, and if it is not, then the relationship, such as it is, may be further defined and changed accordingly.

And what are the R'lyehian's reasons for attempting to enter the Black Gnosis through their own sexual practice? As mentioned earlier, pleasure is clearly a reason, at least on the surface of the experience. But if it stops there, then for the R'lyehian it is a waste of energies, sexual and otherwise. The goal for her is always to transcend, to transform. Is there any deep-sea dive that can equal the one we take while fucking? Is not sexual congress with any partner a profound encounter, confrontation, and eventual assimilation of the Other? If you are going to do it, then by Dagon's Teeth, get it *done.*

Ideally, each sexual encounter needs to have a certain flavour, that of inescapable changes being visited upon all parties: changes to the body, to the mind, to the soul. There should be a point, fearful in its intensity, when a thought not unlike "this is it, I will never be the same after this moment" crosses the R'lyehian's awareness. This point is reached and transcended before one can retreat from the awful import of it.

Naturally, the quest for this particular flavour of sexual experience can take the R'lyehian to some bizarre and fruitful places. It would not be uncommon to find the practicing R'lyehian engaged in, say, bondage and disciplinary sex, fulfilling submissive and dominant roles in a relationship[2],

---

1   Or persons. Group dynamics often lend themselves well to the R'lyehian omnisexual practice, by simple virtue of the variety of possible couplings (triplings? and so on) available in such a scenario.

2   Often performing as a "switch", shuttling back and forth between the two states.

or experimenting with any number of (perceived) transgressive activities[1]. This is not to say that standard vanilla-flavoured coupling cannot partake of the never-the-same-again moment, though it can require more effort.

At this point, it may be insightful to quote the "weird erotica" writer Justine Geoffrey, author of the strange and smutty *Blackstone* series of novellas. In an essay on her creative process[2], she bluntly states...

> *If you're only worrying about how to get him/ her out of your bed so you can sleep because you've got work in the morning, then you're doing it wrong! You should be worrying about how much cosmic energy you're going to have to channel through your ajna chakra as you come, because nothing less than ALL OF IT is going to keep the portal open long enough to get that extra-dimensional beastie you just fucked back through it!*

Miss Geoffrey is fond of her extra-dimensional beasties, I'm given to understand. Whether or not she has actual access to them as potential paramours is not for me to say, but the *principle* expressed here (at least as far as the lengths to which the R'lyehian should be willing to go to achieve transcendence, to enter into union with the Black Gnosis) is utterly sound. And it is this principle that finds a visual expression in what is perhaps one of the more bizarre branches of Mythos-related artwork here in the early years of the 21st Century: tentacle sex[3].

Again, as with PlushCthulhu™, Japan has a lot to answer for when it comes to some of the more tawdry examples of this genre. Japanese *hentai*[4] comic-book images were some of the earliest popular depictions of tentacle

---

1 Again, taking care that any such experimentation does not devolve into mere fetish.

2 *The Unbearable Strangeness of Being: Why I Write Weird Erotica*, which first appeared on the Martian Migraine Press website in April of 2013 and in print later that same year in *Priestess*, a volume of the collected *Blackstone* books. Miss Geoffrey has graciously allowed me to appropriate part of her title for this chapter.

3 There really is no escaping this aspect of the overlap between Lovecraft's Mythos, sexuality, and R'lyehian spirituality. In any discussion, it is the *archeteuthis dux* in the tank, and must be addressed. I shall try to make short work of it here.

4 Directly translated as *perversion*.

sex[1], created largely to get past censors who frowned on graphic depictions of penile penetration of any orifice[2]. Almost without exception, these works (both in print and animation) are crass and unappetizing, though they do display a certain frenzied energy not found in standard pornographic depictions.

Am I here suggesting that the R'lyehian should find such depictions arousing, or helpful in achieving the Black Gnosis during sex? Or, even further along the scale, that the R'lyehian should consider acts of bestiality performed with members of the *genus cephalapoda* a necessary adjunct to their usual sexual practice?

Not at all. Speaking personally, I can't think of any sexual activity less enjoyable, more pointless, and (considering the hooks and beaks, toxins and generally pain-inducing physical attributes common to the anatomy of cephalopods) quite possibly more dangerous than getting squicky with a squid.

But as a visual and metaphoric touchstone for the profound confrontation with the Other that R'lyehian sex practice necessarily entails, tentacle sex is ideal. I believe that this (mainly unconscious) understanding accounts for the rise in popularity of such imagery in recent years: people, men and women, are tired of themselves as Other, and desire the *truly* Other. What could be more Other, sexually, than having ones voids filled with pulsating pseudopods? The squeamish reader will cringe at the image, tremble with a mixture of loathing and amazement at the very idea of attaining unity with something so alien, and it is that cringing response to the image that must be meditated upon during the sexual act, must be entered into and passed through, if the R'lyehian is to understand That Which Is Not within him.

The R'lyehian gazes into the Abyss with awe and affection, his eyes ablaze with the Burning Gaze that lusts for knowledge, for he knows his own transformation is at hand. And as he sinks ever deeper into the enfolding

---

1　Notwithstanding *The Dream of the Fisherman's Wife* (1814), a famous woodcut block print by Hokusai, often cited as inspiration for later innovations in the genre.
2　Toshio Maeda, the creator and artist of the groundbreaking *Urotsukodoji* manga, made this clear in a 2002 interview: "At that time [pre-Urotsuki Doji], it was illegal to create a sensual scene in bed. I thought I should do something to avoid drawing such a normal sensual scene. So I just created a creature. [His tentacle] is not a [penis] as a pretext. I could say, as an excuse, this is not a [penis], this is just a part of the creature. You know, the creatures, they don't have a gender. A creature is a creature. So it is not obscene - not illegal." (Manga Artist Interview Series (Part 1), 2002, www.bigempire.com/sake/manga1.html) Thanks to Robert Derie for the reference.

limbs of his lovers, he is likewise sinking to R'lyeh, where a frenzy of fractal feelers coil and thrash in anticipation of his arrival.

Can anything less than the purest ecstasy await him?

Through Sunset's Gate:
Death and the R'lyehian

"You're going to die, Arnie. Someday, you will face that moment. Regardless of what you believe, at that moment either you will face complete non-existence, which is something you can't possibly imagine, or you will face something even stranger that you also can't possibly imagine. On an actual day in the future, you will be in the unimaginable, Arnie. Set your mind on that."

— David Wong, *John Dies At The End*

All things move toward their end[1]. This, at least, is a universal truth. The fact of your beginning ensured your eventual arrival at your end: such is the inescapable nature of beings embedded in Time and subject to Causality. More than anything else, it is this, the inevitability of Death, that primes the pump of every one of our religions, our sciences, our arts.

---

1   Galaxies, species, individuals, and, yes, cranky books on fringe spirituality.

The power of Religion lies in its time-tested ability to craft mostly convincing and somewhat consoling narratives about what happens to us after Death. Narratives that boil down to one thing: survival. We are promised individual survival beyond that last breath, a survival defined by rewards and punishments of a largely eternal nature. What we are when the conjectured transition is made from life to afterlife is what we shall ever be in the timeless halls of Eternity, and whether the light that shines upon those walls is clear and pure or ruddy with flame and foul is a matter of what we did before the transition. And if we are of a more eastern leaning in our belief, then perhaps a return to the endless cycle of incarnation will be our lot, and another go around the wheel as man or beast or godform, according to (again, but with some small difference) our previous actions.

These are the bedtime stories, the two main narratives our species is fond of[1] and though there are branchings from these (bodily resurrection in a post-Apocalyptic paradise, for one, or a kind of "remembrance" in the mind of God, for another), still the bulk of these beliefs share the same basic memetic DNA: the individual survives Death. You (yes, *you*, that collection of experience and memory that you've come to know and love so much in your, what? Eighty years on the planet? And that if you're lucky...) will not have to stop being you. You will die, but Death is not the end, not for someone as special as *you*.

The various Sciences, each straining in their own direction, are keen to distance themselves from this kind of pie-in-the-sky thought and wish to avoid the worst excesses of Religion. Yet what is the secret longing of Science, if it is not for mastery over the forces that shape, shift, and eventually end our lives? Science pays lip service to the reality of Death, invoking natural cycles and physical laws, entropy and decay, and it does this even as it labours to alter those cycles, subvert those laws. Science seeks to understand and make understandable the world and if it is *pure* Science, then yes, it does that and does it well. Perhaps in some clear R'lyehian future Science will only ever be *pure* but as long as it is practiced by chittering lab-coated apes it will always be enslaved to the (sometime) satisfaction of their whims and the (attempted) eradication of their fears.

Look to the life extension sciences, particularly those with a transhumanist or H+ bent. Cryogenics. Cloning. Robotics, cybernetics. Consciousness duplication and storage. Even space exploration (though not as *en vogue* as it once was) shares with all these myriad probes into the future a whispered dream that is, for all their outward posturing, their true

---

1 Or has been colonized by, after the manner of viral contagion.

fuel: that we might not end. As a species, yes, obviously, but also as individuals. What biotechnologist has not entertained the idea of cloning themselves, either for parts to maintain a failing original body or for an entirely new incorporation? What computer scientist has not wondered just what would be required to upload her own mind and awareness into a machine, approximating immortality via silicon and superconductors? What physicist has not idly fantasized about hitting on the Unified Theory of Everything and the treasure chest of understanding, and power, and possibly transcendence that such a thing would unlock? The eradication of Death, one way or another, is the true goal of Science.

Art, since the moment we pressed ochred hands to cool stone in the Chauvet Caves, has always sought to express and extend the human condition beyond the human body and lifespan. Like the sciences, when the making of Art is pure, then it is perhaps only then that it is about the art itself, and not the artist, but this is rarely the case. One of our first reactions to a piece of great art, if not the very first one, is "who made this?" We marvel at the creation, but wish to know the creator as well. In our modern (or post-modern) era, the artist as cultural hero, as celebrity, is a common enough figure. Fifteen minutes of fame may be the truth of it (as that quite famous artist is known to have quipped), but no artist truly expects or desires anything less than a lifetime's worth of fame, and the great can expect far more. Immortality (of singular vision, of creative power) is the sought-for grail in art. By uniting with the abstract, the personal and conditional is transcended, or at least has the appearance of being transcended.

These, then, are the vectors of Death-denial: the stories we tell about that point after which we cannot possibly know anything, the technologies we build and the research we perform in order to know enough to move that point further ahead in Time or eradicate it altogether, the creative bonds we make with Platonic ideations and thoughtforms in order to sidestep that point entirely. Religion, Science, Art: the pieces we shuffle madly on a game board in the hope of somehow fixing the outcome in our favour.

This chapter is necessarily short, for there is not much that can be said about Death, save that it is the event horizon beyond which we cannot see, comprehend, or intuit. It is unguessable, unnamable, the ultimate Unknown, and our fear of it, as individuals, as a species, is the ultimate Fear. Because of that one day in the future after which we cease to have any days, we are driven to do amazing, terrible, and horrific things.

What, then, is the R'lyehian's response to death? It is much the same as her response to sex, to madness, to life itself: she brings the full power of the Black Gnosis to bear upon it. It is a moment of utter Chill, entered into with a Grin, upon which her Burning Gaze opens a passage into the unknown.

How will the experience of coming to death be any different, the R'lyehian asks herself, than the pulsing edge of the Black Gnosis which she has taken pains to cultivate in her own life on a daily basis[1]? Constant meditation on That Which Is Not, daily affirmations of the Cthulhusattva Vow, nightly oneiric excursions to that super-contextual corpse-city of Dream where death is something to be slept through: the R'lyehian is well-familiar with that incandescent rim beyond which the light of life, reason, and comprehension cannot penetrate. Though it is always an edge-experience, it is still familiar territory.

Thus, the death bed holds no terrors for the R'lyehian, or, if it does, not until that moment before the last intake of breath, where the fear transmutes into an ecstatic fuel for that ultimate launch into the Unknown.

Cultivating the Black Gnosis and applying the lessons learned from it inures us to the base vicissitudes of the moment of death[2], prepares us for the final plunge into the Void, with a malleable and ready mind for whatever awaits us there, beyond the event horizon. In a meaningless, random and chaotic Universe, it is more than likely that there is, in fact, nothing there at all, and Death is truly the End of the World for the individual. The worst fear of the ego is realized, perhaps, and total cessation will be our lot. Making this assumption, though, is as pointless an exercise as assuming a species of personal survival, or that the airy halls of eternity will be entered into.

The R'lyehian assumes nothing of the actual experience of death, save that it will be the climactic encounter with the essence of That Which Is Not, with the beating dark core of the Black Gnosis. The fear or even the anticipation of death, therefore, does not colour the R'lyehian's life at all, causing him to act against others, to lash out and grip and attempt to manipulate that which resists manipulation. Like his life, his death will be what it is: an expression of the ineffable, patient madness that is existence itself.

---

1 Returning, finally, to Lovecraft's fiction, we find that Death, at least for his embattled protagonists, is preferable to madness. Here is the truth of it: as a being embedded in Time, your death is guaranteed. However it plays out, whatever awaits or does not await you on the other side of it, it will be the most profound shift in consciousness, awareness, and being you will ever experience. A little Madness, then, may go a long way towards a successful transition between states.

2 We are reminded here of that wartime aphorism "there are no atheists in foxholes". The R'lyehian, by virtue of a lifetimes practice of the Black Gnosis, spares his friends and family, and indeed, his own self, the shambholic entreaties and mewling protestations that accompany a death wrapped in fear. Like the samurai, the R'lyehian is always ready. The R'lyehian is in many ways already dead: one foot always in the maelstrom of the Black Gnosis.

And if, on the other side of that razor-thin line, the R'lyehian finds, not oblivion, but the unimaginable? Well, she has spent a life in a frenzied dance with the unimaginable. She has lived long nights trading one mask of perception, consciousness, and personality for another. She has made love to the Abyss, rapturously entwined with the Other at every opportunity. She has worked tirelessly to raise R'lyeh in her heart. She is ready. She has always been ready.

Whatever the circumstances of her death, the R'lyehian smiles. The Grin of the Black Gnosis is upon her lips: enigmatic, teasing, a riddle that shares much in common with the famous couplet...

That is not dead, which can eternal lie
and with strange aeons, even Death may die

Those who remain behind cannot know, embedded as we still are in Time and process, whether the stars have turned right for her, whether she has truly been absorbed into the Dream of Cthulhu, but something in that gleeful, anticipatory rictus stirs That Which Is Not within the echo-chambers of our own hollowness and we ache with the wonder and madness of it. The deathbed smile takes a lifetime to produce, and it is perfect.

It is her last gift to the world: a key, and a gate, briefly opened, to R'lyeh itself.

Afterword:
Yes, Meridian,
There Is A Great Cthulhu

Dearest daughter,

The first draft of this book was completed only a few days before you were born. Of all the writing deadlines (self-imposed and otherwise) I've ever had to meet, this was one of the toughest. Would you arrive early? Or ten days late, like your brother? How much time would I have to finish the book, really? Your birthday was a moving target, and it was a close thing, but I made it. It was done (mostly, save for a second, largely unchanged second draft and editing), and two days later, you came into our lives.

Meridian, when you're old enough, you're probably going to read this weird volume of mine; it is, after all, dedicated to you, the little girl I met and whose name I heard called in a dream, long before I met your mum. Now, I've written some weird ones, sure, and I'll likely write weirder, but this book? *When The Stars Are Right* has been a very personal exploration of my own very particular spiritual weirdness.

Honestly, it started off as a joke. A lark. I mean, how could it not? First, this is your dad we're talking about here: I didn't snag your mum on good looks alone. And second, it's a book on the spiritual truth of tentacled monster-gods from beyond Time and Space, gods cobbled together out of whole cloth by a malnourished hack horror writer from the early 20th Century! So, of course it was a joke.

Of *course.*

Only, as I worked my way further into the book, as I thought and wrote and then thought some more, as I examined my life and the things (some of them quite strange - read that intro, it's all true - and a lot of them very sad, which you can ask me about in private) that have happened to me, as I spent time with Yog-Sothoth and Cthulhu, not as pulp horror beasties, but as *principles of being,* and as I searched my heart for what I actually, truly *believed,* it became more and more apparent that I *wasn't* joking. At least, not as much as I thought I was when I first sat down to write the thing. Possibly not at all.

As you grow, and you start to think about things like belief, and faith, and What It All Means Anyway, I know you're going to ask me: "Dad, do you really believe in Cthulhu?" When you ask this, I'm going to have to swallow hard and try not to laugh nervously, which is what my rational, surface-mind is going to want to do. I'm going to have to look you in the eye and I'm going to have to be honest in my reply.

What I say then is going to depend on how old you are when you ask the question. I'm hoping that day comes early (and if you're as smart as your mum, it will), so that I can do like all decent writers and steal - I mean, *paraphrase* - that ancient "Yes, Virginia, There Is A Santa Claus" newspaper editorial. You'll notice I've already cribbed the title for this Afterword. Your dad is pretty shameless.

"Yes, Meridian," I'll say. "I do believe in Cthulhu. He exists as certainly as madness and dreams and the empty spaces between the stars exist, and you know that they abound and give to your life its most fevered ecstasy and dark wisdom. Alas! how *explicably dreary* would be the world if there were no Cthulhu. It would be as dreary as if there were no MERIDIANS..."

And so on with the thieving. But more than that, I believe in the things that study and meditation on Cthulhu and the Great Old Ones have taught me, things that I've tried to put across in this book: the humility of spirit that comes from truly knowing my place in the scheme of things, the wonder of making any kind of sense at all when faced with a senseless existence, the plasticity of the personality, the strange miracle that is language. I mean, there's a *reason* they call it "spelling", my dear, though most have forgotten that reason. The peace (yes, *peace,* deep and still and cool) that comes with the Black Gnosis. I believe that when *all* is madness, there *is* no madness.

I do believe. But I digress. Leaving the blabbering about my R'lyehian faith aside, Meridian, daughter, as long as we're being honest on that day, here's the truth that will be the hardest to tell: your mother and I have brought you into a world of fear.

Human culture has become saturated with fear: fear of ourselves, fear of others. Governments use it as a manipulation tool, the media uses it to sell things, and religion uses it to do both and kill people besides. It's been going on for a long time and they've all become very good at it. It's insane, it's not getting any saner, and it's likely never going to stop. We live and breathe fear every day and as a result we fear *for* things as well, daughter. We fear for the environment, which we're damaging in ways we can't even comprehend, even as we try to save it. We fear for our children. Your mother and I, we fear for you, and for your brother, even as we love you. And we love you *so much.*

Meridian, I've brought you here, invoking you into this fearful world as surely as any pulp era sorcerer, and even as I welcome you with a heart made fierce with love, I despair because I know that you're going to experience pain and you're going to feel fear. I want you to know I will do everything to protect you from the worst of it. Your mother and I will make our home a sanctuary of love and creativity and beauty and joy and fun for you and your brother. You will know love, and compassion, and understanding, which is a lot more than most get, believe me. In this world, love is not guaranteed.

Fear, though? "The oldest and strongest emotion of mankind"? Yes. Sadly, still, and despite all our efforts, despite even the very real love we may receive, fear is guaranteed.

Darling, if you've read this book, then you know: your dad believes that the Universe is, essentially, a meaningless thing. A vast, unknowable Void of heart-stopping, mind-numbing, fearful emptiness, and that the actions of a few billion delusional, spooked monkeys amount to exactly nothing in the grand scheme of whatever-the-hell this Reality is.

The current thinking at the time of your birth is this: our universe is the four-dimensional event horizon of a five-dimensional black hole. We (and by *we* I mean *everything*) are a dead higher-dimensional star. Not even that, we are the gap left in something when something else ceased to be. This is knowledge that does nobody any good, except to show, again, how insignificant we are, how insane all of this is. Suffice it to say, we are hurtling through the black gulfs of the Unknown, clinging to our small speck of dust, hoping to make some sense of things, somehow, and we are, we *are*, but even as we learn more, even as the light of our understanding grows brighter, the wisest of us realize it only reveals more of the Unknown, that primal source of all our fears...

Baby, it's Black Gulfs all the way down.

Your dad is OK with that. I want you to be OK with that, too.

I guess what I'm trying to say here, my love, what I've tried to articulate with the book you're holding now, is this: in a world devoid of meaning, where fear is guaranteed, you've got to *choose what to fear*. Choose it as passionately as you choose what to love.

Because there are going to be a lot of things to be afraid of and a lot of people telling you how and what to fear. Your friends will draw you into their fears for their own solace. Your enemies will inflict theirs on you for their own cruelty. I pray you have many of the former and few of the latter.

Meridian, the world will try to hammer you down with a thousand dull, pointless, meaningless fears. Don't let it. My own mother died in the grip of a fear (twinned with doubt, and the guilt that grew from doubt) that others placed upon her. I'm sorry to say it, and I hope against hope that by the time you read this the situation will have changed, but my father lives in the grip of a lifetimes worth of religiously-induced fear-programming. So much so that, though he lives less than a quarter-hour drive from us, you will likely never meet him. I pity him, because he is missing out on so much, but I also understand him: I lived the same way for a good portion of my adult life and it very nearly killed me, until the day I chose what to fear, and that choosing saved me.

Choose your fear, daughter. Choose it as you would choose your love, your desire, your anger, your sorrow. You won't let others tell you who or what you should love; don't let them tell you what to fear. They do so for their own benefit, not yours. I include myself in that group: yes, I dedicate this book of monsters and terrible things from the gulfs of night to you, but reject it also, reject it completely, if it's not to your liking. I won't mind. But *do* choose. Choose for yourself, and having chosen, own your fear. When you own it, it lifts you up, gifts you with speed, skill, sagacity. Live it, go a little mad with it. Go *more* than a *little* mad, there's a girl. Learn to use it as the tool it is. Above all, learn from it.

Whatever your fears may be, may they be *exquisite*. Not for you the dull, leaden fears of this world, that serve only to weigh down and kill slowly. May your fears be sharp. May they move you from the very deepest part of your being to do incredible things, things that clarify your mind and steel your heart, that open you to new experiences and insights into yourself, into others, into the world. Be mad for your fear, for in madness we glimpse a little, off in the distance, of what makes us great and we then move toward that greatness. May your fear, like your love, be a darkly shining path to a deeper gnosis.

And know that I will never belittle your fears, or scoff at them, or tell you not to be afraid. I know how valuable they are, how much a part of you they will be. Never be ashamed of them, never feel that you can't speak of them, or share them. Know that I will always honour and respect your fears, and help you to understand them, or, if they cannot be understood, help you to sit with them and find peace in their thrashing, incomprehensible midst. I swear to always "keep it R'lyeh" with you, my sweet girl.

I'm going to be there for you, for as long as I can, as you walk that path into the Unknown. We can walk it together, Meridian. You and I, and your mother and brother. If there is meaning at all in the Universe, then perhaps it is there, in the hand a father holds out for his daughter to grasp in the darkness.

Welcome to the big scary world, daughter. I love you.

Fhtagn.

Recommended Reading

Perhaps it should go without mentioning, but it is nearly always instructive to read the collected works of H. P. Lovecraft from time to time. The early readings during adolescence and young adulthood are often powerful experiences in and of themselves, and if the reader is "sensitive" (or, at least, *imagines* themselves to be so), then Lovecraft's tales have a tendency to hit a certain sweet spot in the developing mind. A R'lyehian trigger, perhaps? I count myself in that group, naturally. Readings in later years are similarly rewarding, and often for far different reasons. If this book has revealed anything at all about the strange efficacy of Lovecraft's prose, than it is the ease with which one may read between his lines. Returning to Innsmouth and Arkham, Dunwich and Boston at intervals in life, weighted down with new insights and experiences, serves to open further avenues of understanding in the Old Gentleman's fiction.

Lovecraft's collected works have seen wide print throughout the 20th Century and continue to enjoy publishing success into the present day. Indeed, the tide of Lovecraftiana shows no sign of ever letting up: the act of finding his books is as simple as an Amazon search, or a quick browse at any bookstore, new and used. I have a fondness for the ratty old Ballantine paperbacks with the John Holmes covers. For those inclined to read their books in electronic form, however, I highly recommend visiting the webmaster over at cthulhuchick.com. Ruth has a Masters in Library and Information Science, with a specialization in archives, and has compiled the complete works of Lovecraft for free download to your Nook or Kindle or similarly enabled device.

I would be remiss if I did not mention the criticism and histories compiled by long time Lovecraft scholar S. T. Joshi. Like the work of HPL himself, to set everything Joshi has written about his subject down here would be exhausting. A complete list may be found at stjoshi.org

Robert M. Price is another Lovecraft scholar and editor of no small note who has been at this game for years. If you've yet to acquaint yourself with his amusing and erudite writing, I can think of no better place to start than the introduction to an anthology of tales he edited for Chaosium

Press, *The Nyarlathotep Cycle: Stories About the God of a Thousand Forms* (1996). In many ways, my long-ago reading of this clever breakdown of the Mighty Messenger's possible avatars in the major religions of the world, and Price's deft existential reversal of the final shattering revelation that closes Lovecraft's *The Shadow Over Innsmouth*, is the germ at the heart of this book, the irritant at the centre of my humble little pearl here.

Michel Houellebecq's *H. P. Lovecraft: Against the World, Against Life* (first published in English in 2005) gets down and uncomfortably close to the raw, throbbing nub of Lovecraft's obsessions: his fears, racism, and profound *anomie*, and, as such, provides the R'lyehian with a kind of negative role-model in the man himself. Though the R'lyehian dresses his thought and practice in Lovecraft's trappings, the *actual thinking* of the man is alternately worrisome, laughable, and sad. There but for the gothic majesty and grace of Cthulhu go we: Houellebecq's excellent work holds a dark mirror up to our psyche as we make ourselves R'lyehian.

Attempting to say anything at all about *Cyclonopedia: Complicity with Anonymous Materials* (re.press, 2008), a work of "theory-fiction" by the Iranian speculative-realist Reza Negarestani, is, as the title suggests, an exercise in complicity with the Void itself: before even describing what it's about (wHole complexes? sentient war machines? oil as active planetary consciousness?) the text severely disorients and radically reformats the reader, mapping itself onto the infinite surface area of the gaps in their own knowledge. Mythos deities are here and alive within the pages of *Cyclonopedia*, and though the book rests tentatively just this side of comprehensibility, it is as close to a genuine *Necronomicon* as I have yet to encounter, a true tome of That Which Is Not. Utterly baffling and monstrous, as all truly challenging philosophy should be. Worth owning, worth entering and being entered by.

A gentler entrance into the philosophical underpinning of Lovecraft's fiction may be found in Graham Harman's *Weird Realism: Lovecraft and Philosophy* (Zero Books, 2012). Harman deals with the "gaps" in Lovecraft's writing and the existential tension that arises in those spaces between concepts: essentially, the thrill of the unknowable on the edge of knowing itself, a very R'lyehian experience indeed.

And finally, I'm just going to put this here without commentary (besides the admonition "if you have not read this, then you really, *really* should"): *Book of the SubGenius* (McGraw-Hill, 1983)

Acknowledgements

The names on this list are numerous, but first and foremost I would like to thank my wife, Sasha Prynn, for her unfailing support and encouragement throughout the writing process, both during the creation of this book and others. It is perhaps an old saw to play, but living with a writer does have its challenges; living with a genre writer who suffers a pronounced mystical kink in his psychological and emotional makeup is surely a special subset of those challenges.

Jordan Stratford was very generous with both editorial services and advice (as well as that spiffy Foreweird!) and his wisdom and experience in things both spiritual (Gnosticism, alchemy, *life!*) and practical (the publishing industry, design, *life!*) are invaluable to me. I am honoured and humbled to call him friend, and continually chuffed that he allows me to pick his brain over like the primitive scavenger that I am.

Editors Ross E. Lockhart and Silvia Moreno-Garcia entered my life around the time I started writing *When The Stars Are Right,* and their years of experience and behind-the-scenes insights into book and magazine production, the writing process, and promotion, proved to be lessons I will remember always.

Thanks, too, to the writers who are, in my opinion, "keepin' it R'lyeh", and who have served to inspire my creativity and clarify my thinking *vis a vis* all things Lovecraftian in literature and in life: Nick Mamatas, Laird Barron, Richard Gavin, Bryan Thao Worra, Wilum Hopfrog Pugmire, Molly Tanzer, and Nathan Ballingrud. Robert Derie was also a consistent and reliable source of all manner of Lovecraftian minutia ranging from the scholarly to the trashy.

All the "Weird Twitter" followers of my account, @Cthulhusattva, who endured/enjoyed a long-ish period of excerpts from the book. R'lyehian spirituality is heady enough without receiving it in a 140-character drip-feed in the middle of the night. I'm told that's when WeirdTwitter is most active though, and I appreciate all the support and strange avenues of thought my interaction with that medium and its (admittedly nebulous) users produced.

Though the "H. P. Lovecraft's 120th Birthday Celebration and Cthulhu-riffic Cabaret" I created and hosted is years in the past by now, a special thanks to all the weirdos and assorted Lovecraft geeks who made it out to that most strange and frantic of nights at the Solstice Café in Victoria, BC. The quasi-revival feel of that evening certainly provided the germ of inspiration which led to this book. There was a kind of glory in that room that night, manifested in a way that only a great audience can, and I only hope I have managed to adequately transmute a fraction of that glory into book form. Thanks also to David Cardinal and shayne avec i grec for opening their Solstice space to me. They tell me that having a 12' wide *papier maché* and fiberglass Cthulhu head hanging from the rafters was good for business, and Dagon bless 'em for saying so.

Finally, thanks to Michael Lee Macdonald, the talented artist/illustrator whose work very literally graces these pages with wonder and raw primitivism. Michael and I both live in the same town, but did not meet until I stumbled upon his "daily draw" page on Facebook. His art is amazing, his company enjoyable, and his proximity a stroke of excellent luck. In a lot of ways, I consider his work in these pages to be the best thing about the book and I can't thank him enough for his early readings of the text, his critiques and insights, and the inspired art that arose from them.

About the Author

Scott R Jones is a writer, spoken-word artist, and naturalized sorcerer. His fiction and poetry has appeared in *Broken City, Innsmouth Magazine, Cthulhu Haiku II,* and *Andromeda Spaceways Inflight Magazine.* His short story collections *Soft From All The Blood* and *The Ecdysiasts,* as well as a poetry chapbook, *R'lyeh Sutra* (writing as skawt chonzz), are available from Martian Migraine Press. He lives in Victoria, BC, with his wife and two children.

About Martian Migraine Press

We are an independent Canadian micro-press with a focus on the weird, unusual and occasionally transgressive. Fiction that plays with boundaries before ignoring them altogether; erotica with dark humour and a taste for the outré, and poetry for people from other planets. Martian Migraine books are available almost exclusively in e-reader formats through the usual fine online retailers, although we sometimes make forays into producing physical books and chapbooks in limited press runs. Mostly when we're feeling nostalgic.

A note to users of social media...

We here at Martian Migraine Press hope you've
enjoyed *When The Stars Are Right* enough
to want to talk about it with others. To that
end, may we suggest the following selec-
tion of fine and provocative hashtags:

#KeepingItRlyeh

#BlackGnosis

#Cthulhusattva

Also, if you've reviewed the book for your own
publication(s), or would like Mr Jones to appear on
your podcast, do drop us a line to let us know where
your review appears, or to arrange an interview.

We can be reached via email at
info@martianmigrainepress.com or
tweet at us @MartianMigraine

Be sure to check out these other Martian Migraine Press titles...

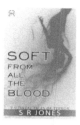

SOFT FROM ALL THE BLOOD
by Scott R Jones

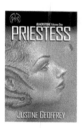

PRIESTESS
the collected BLACKSTONE Erotic Series, Volume One
by Justine G

R'LYEH SUTRA
by skawt chonzz

martianmigrainepress.com

Follow us on Twitter @MartianMigraine